Dewitt C. Greer

King of the Highway Builders

Richard Morehead

Distinguished Texans Series

Sponsored by Texas Historical Foundation

EAKIN PRESS ᴇᴘ Fort Worth, Texas
www.EakinPress.com

DEDICATION

To men and women who have built Texas,
of which its highway department
is a shining example of integrity, loyalty,
and ability in public service.

Contents

Foreword

This biography of Dewitt C. Greer is an inspiration of A. Sam Waldrop, who came to full appreciation of the character, talent and contributions of the man during the three years they served together on the Texas Highway Commission from 1978 to 1981.

Late in 1982, while still chairman of the commission, Waldrop invited me to meet with him, Engineer-Director Mark G. Goode, and Tom Taylor of the department's information staff to discuss the idea. It was accepted without hesitation on my part, because I had long been a friend and admirer of the leader who made the Texas highway system the envy of the world, an achievement which Greer always insisted must be shared with many others, particularly the department's loyal and dedicated employees.

Next John Ben Shepperd, whom I knew as attorney general of Texas, accepted Waldrop's suggestion that the Texas Historical Foundation sponsor the project as the first in a "Distinguished Texans Series."

Edwin Eakin of the Eakin Press, who has done much to encourage the writing of books about Texas and Texans, eagerly agreed to publish the book, so the project was launched.

Several of Greer's friends, mostly colleagues from his days as chief administrator and later as commission member-chairman, volunteered support so the achievements of this remarkable public official could be preserved in book form.

These included Mr. and Mrs. Waldrop, Robert Dedman, Reagan Houston, Judge Hal Woodward, Garrett

Morris, H. C. Petry, Marshall Formby, E. H. Thornton Jr., and Charles E. Simons — all Greer-era commissioners. Others are Robert C. Lanier, the present commission chairman, John R. Butler, B. R. Jones, M. L. Dalton, and H. B. Zachry, all of whom knew Greer well and appreciated his service and ability.

The department, which since 1975 has been titled "State Department of Highways and Public Transportation" (a name Greer and other old-timers disliked) assisted the author immensely. Especially helpful was Clara Bewie, who served fifty years with the commission, mostly as its secretary. Clara knew about everybody who worked for the department and shared the information gladly.

Each of Greer's successors as engineer-director contributed information: J. C. (Ding) Dingwall, B. L. (Luther) DeBerry, and Mark G. Goode, all products of the Greer School of Highway Construction and Honorable Public Service. The admiration of those who knew Greer best is so overwhelming it was impossible to find any negative views. One observer suggested the only thing remaining would be to "canonize" the subject.

Thanks go to Tom Taylor and his staff for much assistance and to Texas A.&M. University for sharing the fine doctoral dissertation by John David Huddleston, "Good Roads for Texas: A History of the Texas Highway Department, 1917-1947."

Richard Morehead
November 1983
Austin, Texas

1

King of the Highway Builders

More than any person in history, Dewitt Carlock Greer, deserves the crown of King of the Roads.

The modest Texan, whose life closely paralleled America's golden age of motor vehicles, saw seventy thousand miles of all-weather highways built to replace dusty trails and roads which became impassable when wet. Millions of motor vehicles took over tasks previously performed by railroads, waterways, horses, mules, and even oxen.

Near the peak of his distinguished career, Greer was described:[1]

"Dewitt C. Greer hardly looks like a man spending a million dollars a day.[2] During the noon hour, Greer is likely to be found dining in an Austin cafeteria. His diet, dress, manner, speech and deeds are conservative.

"Yet Dewitt Greer, Texas Highway Engineer, holds one of the biggest, most creative positions in government. He views his career correctly as much more than dollars, steel and concrete. A bridge or a pavement to him is like a canvas to an artist. Roads mean moving people and products, the building of industry, and human touches like carrying the kids to school. . . .

"Greer loves his work, and he recommends government jobs to the younger generation — in contrast to advice often given by others. . . . If he was starting his life
anew, Greer would follow his same career. He wouldn't
trade places with anybody. . . ."

To Greer, highways and buildings were life itself. He
spent more than sixty years at the task, including fifty-
five years with the Texas Highway Department, later renamed Texas Department of Highways and Motor Transportation (a title Greer and other old-timers largely ig-
nored).

One of Greer's few regrets was that he was not born
in Texas, a fact which he is reluctant to discuss.

His parents, Samuel Rufus Greer and Mary Lou
Carlock, lived briefly in Shreveport, where Dewitt was
born July 27, 1902.

The father was a drug products wholesaler, and
when the infant was three weeks old, the family moved
back to Pittsburg, in Camp County, East Texas, which
Greer calls his home. It was a pretty town of trees and
flowers, handicapped by the muddy streets of the frequent rains. Pittsburg later grew to nearly four thousand population, with fine highways, including one dedicated in 1966 to its famous son, then in his twenty-sixth
year as head of the Texas Highway Department.

Greer's father later became a banker at Pittsburg,
then in Tyler, and in both places was a civic leader.

"Dad was a banker, but he made us (sons) work,"
Greer recalled in 1983, living in semi-retirement in an attractive home on Mount Barker in Austin.

S. Marcus Greer, Dewitt's older brother who became
a prominent Houston banker, said of their boyhood:

"I was several years older than he was and therefore
I felt a little more grown up at the age of ten or twelve
than he . . . When he was a little kid, I found him quite a
pest in wanting to go everywhere I went, principally
squirrel or rabbit hunting with our dog, Fritz.[3]

"Almost every day, both of us got out of school about three p.m. We lived just a block from the school so in a few minutes I was home — had my shotgun and headed for the woods. Dewitt trailed behind me with Fritz and gave me a little trouble; however, he was a help before the hunt was over. If I killed a rabbit or a squirrel he was happy to carry whatever game I killed during that day's hunting. So I soon got to the point where not only would I tolerate him but was glad to have him along as a retriever. . . ."

Dewitt insisted that "work was my hobby" later in life. He did occasionally "go hunting" with friends, but seldom fired a gun. He enjoyed camp life and hunted quail some time on the ranch of his longtime friend, Dolph Briscoe of Uvalde (governor and state legislator, a staunch supporter of highway building). On such trips, Greer passed up invitations to hunt the big South Texas whitetail deer, which abound in that area.

The best-known Greer hunting story occurred years later. While hunting quail with a friend in South Texas, the companion fired at a rising covey of birds and one pellet ricocheted off a fence wire, striking Greer in the rear.

"You SOB!" the wounded victim exclaimed. "You just shot the head of the Texas Highway Department in the butt."

Strong words from a mild-mannered man. A surgeon in the hunting party removed the errant pellet from Greer in camp that night with little harm done, a truly happy end.

Another quail hunting story is told by Charles F. Hawn, a former highway commissioner, who visited Briscoe's Catarina Ranch with Greer and other friends. While others hunted elsewhere, Briscoe dispatched a ranch hand to help Greer hunt quail.

After awhile, the host and Hawn drove over to see how Greer was faring.

"We came up behind Dewitt," Hawn recalled. "He was walking down the road with his gun out front, ready to shoot. Several blue quail were following right behind him. It was a funny sight."

Of his early life, Greer wrote this account:
"My mother was a Carlock and spent her early years in Winnsboro. On the death of her mother she came to live on Pitts Hill with her relatives . . . , who I believe were among the founders of Pittsburg. My father came from down near Gilmer with his widowed mother and she opened Mrs. Greer's Seminary for Girls in Pittsburg. As they reached the proper age, they were married. . . .

"By some queer turn of fate, I was born in Shreveport, where my parents lived for a brief stay before returning to Pittsburg at the time I had achieved the ripe old age of three weeks . . . My entire early life was spent in Pittsburg since I have no memory whatever of Shreveport.

"All of my schooling up to and through graduation from high school was in the public schools of Pittsburg. I rather doubt there was anything spectacular in my high school career. . . . Carroll Spearman was the most brilliant of the boys, and I may have run second. I am not even sure about this.

"During my high school days, I heard the call of music and enlisted in the high school and town bands, starting out on an instrument called the Alto (French horns as they might be known today). I later transferred to the trombone since this seemed to be more spectacular and the girls liked it better. . . .

"I sold and delivered the *Dallas Times-Herald* early every morning before I went to school. I swept out the First State Bank in the spare time I had between the paper route and school time.

"My good father followed a worthwhile basic principle that an idle mind is the devil's workshop. . . . He always seemed to find me a job in any spare time I might have after school or in the summer months.

"I worked at Huey's Drug Store ... Hill's Grocery Store ... the peach-packing sheds ... at Mr. Prince's Box Factory ... at the sweet potato sheds and other endeavors.

"This seemed not only to keep me out of devilment but also helped pay my incidental expenses and pay for a little stock in the First State Bank that my father was thoughtful enough to buy for me on credit. ..."

When Dewitt was about twelve years old, his father bought their first automobile, a Maxwell touring car. "Touring cars" with open sides and soft tops which sometimes could be folded back, convertible-style, were popular for the few who could afford motor vehicles and knew how to drive. Some of the early cars came with breakable glass windshields, but glass-enclosed sedans were scarce until safety glass was invented in the late 1920s.

While Sam Greer served as mayor of Pittsburg, Main Street became its first paved street.

"It was curved around a fallen tree," Dewitt chuckled later.

Besides serving as mayor, Greer's father was active in Democratic party politics. Besides Dewitt and Marcus, the Greers had a third son, Robert, a U.S. Army engineer who died in Japan during World War II after being captured in the Philippines, and a daughter, Eoline, now deceased. Robert Greer lies buried in Arlington National Cemetery.

From his father, Greer adopted a lifelong policy of frugality and wise investment.

"My old daddy told me: 'Son, never borrow money — lend money,'" said Greer.

The son "almost never borrowed anything — never used credit cards," he told this writer.

Greer's closeness with money became legendary. He considered the trait a compliment.

Once while hunting with two friends, some ducks flew over and the other two fired, knocking down one bird and winging another which fell some distance away. Greer didn't fire a shot, but took after the wounded birds with a stick and killed both.

Tom Collier of Austin, one of the hunters, told the story to Helen, Greer's wife.

"I told her Dewitt killed two ducks and hadn't fired a shot," said Collier.

"That sounds like him," Helen responded. "When he lost his ball, he gave up golf."

Greer was as careful with the taxpayers' money in the Highway Department, as with his own. One fellow-worker described Greer as "a tightwad" on spending public or private funds. He served as treasurer for the First Methodist Church in Austin, and followed a business-like policy there. After retiring from the Highway Department as a commissioner member-chairman in 1981, Greer continued to serve as a director and head of the Trust Committee of the American Bank in Austin, taking a personal interest in its operation.

Shyness marked Greer's early life. In high school, he decided to court a local girl, but was afraid to tell his parents. So he took his horn, announced he was going to band practice, hid the instrument in a hedge down the street and proceeded to visit the object of his affection on her front porch. He never told the girl about hiding his horn.

Until Greer met and married Helen Colton of Athens, several years after he finished Texas A&M, Greer's social life with girls was limited.

As a senior student, Greer had his only date at Texas A&M. He invited Maurine Smith of Pittsburg to the annual dance given by senior cadets. A dormitory was vacated by male students to make room for the visiting girls.

"She stayed for the dances," Greer reported. "Thirty days after she got home, she married. It was the last time I ever saw her. That's how good I was at courting."

[1] Richard M. Morehead, *Dallas Morning News*, Sept. 15, 1963.
[2] About four million dollars daily in 1983, Comptroller Bob Bullock's report, May 1983.
[3] Letter to the author, Apr. 25, 1983.

2

College Station

Dewitt Greer's first trip to Texas Agricultural and Mechanical College at College Station was less than a triumphant entry for the sixteen-year-old small-town lad.

"The majority of the boys in our graduating class decided with me to attend Texas A&M," he recounted many years later.

"We were all leaving on the Cotton Belt (railroad) in the wee hours of the night on our first venture into the outside world. I joined my mother and father in the careful setting of the alarm clock to be at the station well ahead of the time for departure."

Unfortunately, the alarm clock failed.

"When we woke up, the Cotton Belt already had gone with my classmates heading for Big Sandy and Texas A&M. Sadness and disappointment prevailed."

Since Pittsburg had two railroads at the time, Greer and his father went to the Cotton Belt station with a wheelbarrow, picked up his trunk, and wheeled it several blocks to the other line. In the middle of the night. Greer's father discovered (by waking several friends in Pittsburg) that the other railroad carried passengers to

Greenville "and from there to several other points and eventually to A&M after probably a couple of days' travel.

"I did board this train, whatever its name was (and) eventually get to A&M where I was received with doubtful enthusiasm by my colleagues and classmates, due to my dereliction."

Despite this unspectacular arrival, in his four years at College Station, Greer became an Aggie to the core. He graduated with scholastic honors in 1923, and with a commission in the United States Army as a second lieutenant of infantry.

Greer started to college when he was sixteen years old, "too young" he commented later.

Freshmen at A&M then were prohibited even from riding the trolley to Bryan.

"The freshmen had to stay home and keep house," Greer explained.

The shrewdness and diplomacy for which Greer later became noted were honed in his first year of college, in the lowest rank of the powerful corps.

"It was a liberal education," he said of the hazing.

"They used long paddles. It taught me how to argue myself out of a beating. Later in life I was able to talk myself out of lots of trouble."

When an upper-classman approached to discipline Greer, the slender, five-foot-ten freshman urged a reasonable approach by the usually larger Aggie.

"Let's talk this thing over," Greer would say. "What good would it do either one of us for you to beat my butt? Why not let me make your bed for a week?"

Usually, it worked.

While a freshman, Dewitt had a visit from his brother Marcus, then an upper-classman at the University of Texas at Austin.

"I was to spend only one night with him, but he informed me at the last minute he had to go to the cotton fields to be hazed by the upper-classmen," Marcus recalled. "I got a good night's sleep, but he did not. In spite of the hazing, Dewitt loved the school and completed his college career with honors."

On another occasion, Greer's military company was ordered by Colonel Ike Ashburn, the corps commandant, to move from the dormitory into tents on a nearby mud flat. Greer disliked the black mud and surreptitiously returned to his dormitory to sleep. Discovered by the commandant, Greer was ordered back to the tents with his troops.[1]

"Colonel Ike" a beloved figure at Aggieland, later became head of the Texas Good Roads Association and Greer's staunch friend and supporter.

Years after Greer graduated, A&M officials stopped the hazing of freshman, a move which Greer approved.

In college, music was Greer's major extracurricular activity. He played trombone in the band and made football trips to other campuses.

On one such trip, traveling aboard a special train, Greer said that in Austin "some University of Texas students wrapped my trombone around my neck."

During his time at College Station, where the famous Dana X. Bible then coached football, Greer never saw the Aggies lose a game for the first three years. Bible later went to Nebraska and to the University of Texas to continue his record of winning teams.

Dewitt said his father spent two thousand dollars sending him to college.

"I paid him back," the son added.

Greer intended to become an electrical engineer when he enrolled at A&M, mainly because he was good in mathematics and with electrical gadgets. Once at Pittsburg, he tried to mechanize the family ice-cream freezer so it wouldn't need hand-cranking on Sundays.[2]

He turned to civil engineering after working on a summer road construction job in Pittsburg.

"I liked the whole idea of outdoor work, engineering

and the status symbol that went with it — lace-up boots," he explained.

"It was easy for me (civil engineering and highway courses). I made straight A's in math, physics, and all my engineering courses. I never made an F but I dern near flunked public speaking. None of the engineering students could see any need for such stuff."[3]

In retrospect, Greer's shyness and lack of enthusiasm for public speaking didn't stop him from becoming a very effective speaker.

As state highway administrator, Greer was called upon to attend numerous ribbon cuttings for opening new highways and bridges and on other occasions.

"Nobody has yet perfected a mechanism for cutting down the number and length of speeches at ribbon cuttings, but reporters are always happy when D. C. Greer is the honor guest," the *Dallas Morning News* once commented. "He says something appropriate, and more appropriately, he says it and sits down."

An unnamed official of the Western Association of State Highway Officials added:

"I sure like that fellow (Greer). Whenever he says anything at these meetings, it's worth listening to."[4]

Besides the band and cadet corps, Greer tried out for the track team, but never made it. He attended two summer camps of the Reserve Officers Training Corps at Fort Logan, Colorado, and maintained his second lieutenant's commission for several years afterward.

Greer's roommate in Texas A&M was Otto P. Weyland, nicknamed "Nuts." After Weyland became a four-star Air Force general, the veteran of two wars, Greer kept in touch with his old friend and visited him in retirement in San Antonio, where Weyland died.

"After he got to be a four-star general, he didn't like to be called 'Nuts,'" Greer chuckled.

Dewitt's nickname "Dee" continued through his life

from boyhood and A&M friends, although few Highway
Department employees ever addressed him as other than
"Mr. Greer" after he became the top man.

¹ Marshall Formby, letter to the author, Mar. 8, 1983.
² Golden Anniversary, Texas Highway Department history, 1917-
1967, p. 35.
³ Ibid.
⁴ Ibid.

3

Engineer Greer
and His Convict Crew

As with his arrival at A&M, Greer's debut into engineering after graduation was hardly spectacular.

He applied verbally for a job in highway construction at Paris with a state employee named Dockery, and was turned down.[1]

Greer's father, ambitious to see his son get ahead, (without Dewitt's knowledge) wrote to Chairman R. M. Hubbard of the Texas Highway Commission saying his department needed someone like "his brilliant young son."[2]

"Fortunately, my father got the brush-off," Greer related.

The reason the brush-off was all right was that the State Highway Department, especiallly engineers and top officials, were becoming embroiled in a controversy involving the Governors Ferguson. In 1924, Mrs. Miriam A. Ferguson was elected for her first term.

The law creating the Texas Highway Department was passed by the Legislature April 4, 1917, the same day the United States Congress declared war on Germany in World War I. It was signed by Governor James E. Ferguson (husband of Miriam A.) before he was removed from office by scandals in August the same year.

"The bill created a State Highway Commission and office of state highway engineer; directed the department to cooperate with the federal government in utilizing funds appropriated by the Congress for road improvement, it authorized the use of state convicts in road construction; it charged the Agricultural and Mechanical College of Texas and the University of Texas to give aid to the department; and it provided for the registration of motor vehicles and the fees to be charged per registration."[3]

Although Gov. James E. Ferguson favored the legislation, he had reservations about the motor vehicle.

The governor recommended that the Legislature create the new agency, and finance it with registration fees, but "Farmer Jim," as the Temple man was known, added:

"In order that the general public may enjoy the use of the public highways with reasonable safety, I am in favor of a law making it a jail penalty to run an automobile more than ten miles an hour in any incorporated town or more than twenty-four miles an hour on a county road. There is an imperative demand that the speed maniac be dealt with in some drastic measure."[4]

The Highway Department was far from a happy place during its infancy, with bickering among the commissioners and dispute over how far the state could get into highway matters previously the exclusive domain of counties and cities.

Pat M. Neff, who succeeded William P. Hobby, Sr., as governor in 1921 was friendly toward developing the idea of building a state highway system, linking up the disconnected strips of county roads, almost entirely unpaved.

During Neff's second term, 1923-25, the Legislature adopted a constitutional amendment for the purpose, and passed a one cent per gallon gasoline tax to finance the program, but opposition within the State Capitol and county seats brought legal action halting these measures.

Friction over contracts also had developed between A. R. Losh, the Texas district engineer for the United States Bureau of Public Roads, and Gibb Gilchrist, who became the Texas Highway Department's chief administrator. Former Gov. James E. Ferguson sided with the federal engineer, a position supported by Mrs. Ferguson when she was elected in 1924 to succeed Neff the following year. There also were charges of favoritism and corruption in letting of State Highway Department contracts.

When Dewitt Greer came into the engineer job market, the State Highway Department was under a heavy cloud.

Gibb Gilchrist, who became Greer's close friend and mentor, liked to claim later that the newly graduated Texas Aggie didn't get hired immediately by the Highway Department because he and the commission wanted "to make him work his way up the hard way."⁵

In any case, Greer took what he described as "a rather outstanding job with a highway contractor (Cocke and Turner . . . later Cocke and Braden) at $110 a month."

A road was being built toward Winnsboro, out by Lessburg and Newsome.

"Being a brilliant young engineer," he related with a smile, "I thought I'd soon be boss of the outfit."⁶

It didn't quite turn out that way. The first two weeks, he filled out time sheets and payrolls.

"But the next week the boss told me to report to work in overalls. He put me to work riding the rear end of an asphalt distributor — operating the burners and opening the valves," said Greer. "The stuff splashed all over me. That job soon had me wondering what I'd gone to college for."

His next assignment was operating a rock crusher, another dirty job.

"You know, I never did get to be superintendent of a job. But I learned the hard way about building highways. I also learned how obnoxious a supervising engineer can be. This later proved to be of great value."

After his introduction into highway construction, Greer took what he termed a "pansy planting" job in Dallas with landscape architect Homer Fry, developing the exclusive Turtle Creek residential area. Greer's engineering task was to design and build swimming pools and driveways.

As a landscape engineer, the boyish-looking Greer was in demand.

"... I would listen to what the ladies wanted," Greer explained. "And without wasting any time, I'd put their ideas into motion...improve on them, but never change."[7]

— Another indication of one reason Dewitt Greer became such a successful negotiator with legislators, governors, county officials and others in putting across his views without being disagreeable.

... After Dallas and Turtle Creek's wealthy clients, Greer switched abruptly into supervisor-landscape engineer for the new Texas State Parks Board, sponsored by Governor Neff.

Greer's assignment: supervising twenty-six state prison "honor" trusty inmates preparing the site for a park on the Guadalupe riverbank near Boerne in Kendall county.

They called it the "Pat Neff Honor Camp."[8]

Before Greer became the parks board's engineer, the convict crew had built the site for the first park built and operated by the State of Texas.

It was "Mother Neff Park" on the Leon River in Coryell County. Mrs. I. E. Neff, the governor's mother, willed six acres for the project, which was later expanded greatly.

"Trusty" convicts guarded by a Texas Ranger worked on Mother Neff's park site.

When Dewitt Greer became the state parks department's first engineer, his workmen consisted of twenty-six convicts — murderers, rapists, thieves, and bootleggers, all considered trustworthy enough to be allowed outside "The Walls" at Huntsville without fleeing their guards or committing further crimes.

One drawback to Greer's new position, besides the background of his workmen, was the lack of any appropriation to pay the engineer's salary. Governor Neff hoped the money would be forthcoming.

It never was. Greer spent nearly a year working with his convicts improving park sites at Boerne and Fredericksburg. He still hasn't been paid.

He remembers the experience without regret.

"It was the most interesting year of my life," said Greer. "I ate convict food, wore their clothes, slept in their tents . . . and never received a penny for it."⁹

The first day and night, a Texas Ranger stayed at the riverbank tent camp, then the slender engineer was alone with his squad of convict strangers.

"When the Ranger left," said Greer, "we sat around the camp fire and I told these men: 'You are honor convicts. If any of you want to leave, you can borrow my suitcase — but if they catch you, you'll be back behind the Walls.'¹⁰

"None of them left (without permission).

"After about a year, the Fergusons pardoned all my convicts. I'd lend each one of them my suitcase as he went home. The last one kept the suitcase."

Mrs. Ferguson became governor in January 1925, and by June Greer's honor camp was empty. So he left too. The Fergusons were lenient on pardon policy, and all of Greer's men had demonstrated they could be trusted and would work.

It was a memorable time for the young engineer. Occasionally, the prisoners boarded the camp truck and went with Greer to San Antonio, where they could see motion pictures free at local theaters.

Once, Greer's charges backed away from reboarding the truck to return to camp. He admits being shaken.

"I thought I had trouble," said Greer.

Then one man came forward and said:

"Mr. Greer, we need to go to a whorehouse. We know some women at one here in San Antonio."

Greer chose what seemed his wisest course.

"I went with them," he said. "They didn't have any money, and they didn't cause any trouble. After awhile, they all came back to the truck and we went back to camp."

Fond memories surround Greer's year with the convicts.

"We'd sit around the campfire shooting the bull," he said. "They talked, and I'd listen. The trusties would talk about their days of crime, laugh over their mistakes, and discuss how they wouldn't get caught next time."

All of Greer's convicts were white men.

"Looking back," said Greer, "the idea (of using convict labor to build parks) wasn't a bad idea. The men liked the work. They were good workers. They enjoyed living in tents outdoors. Their ages ranged from the twenties to about forty-five. Afterward, I corresponded with them for quite a few years. So far as I know, none of them ever went back to prison."

The men didn't work on Sundays. They were allowed to swim and fish in the river, and "loafed around camp."

The camp became a local tourist attraction. On Sunday afternoon, families of the area occasionally would drive by to show the children "the convicts."

"The men decided to put on a show for these people," Greer chuckled. "They put the ugliest convict on a long chain, and tied him to a tree. When a car came by, he'd make a run toward it to the end of his chain."

"It would scare hell out of the gawkers and tickle the convicts."

While operating the Boerne project, Greer drew plans for Bastrop State Park, which later was built by the Civilian Conservation Corps, a program for unemployed youth established by the federal government during the depression of the 1930s.

While the Boerne camp lasted, Greer used equipment furnished by the prison system, and had a convict cook, who bought fresh fruit, chickens, and eggs from local growers. Greer suspected that the convict-cook also managed to buy bootleg whiskey while on these shopping trips, but never caused any trouble.

When the last convict departed, Greer gave a neighboring rancher the camp's remaining food, sent the equipment back to Huntsville, and reapplied for a job as landscape engineer with Homer Fry in Dallas.

"I never had any money while I was at Boerne," Greer explained. "I borrowed one hundred dollars from a Boerne bank to get out of town."

[1] Interview with DCG, Jan. 13, 1983.

[2] Golden Anniversary history.

[3] "Good Roads for Texas: A History of the Texas Highway Department, 1917-1947," a doctoral dissertation by John David Huddleston, Texas A&M University, 1981.

[4] Ibid., quoting from The House Journal, Texas Legislature, 1917 regular session.

[5] Golden Anniversary history, p. 36.

[6] Golden Anniversary history, p. 34.

[7] *Austin American-Statesman*, Charles E. Green, 1940.

[8] Golden Anniversary history, p. 37.

[9] Interview with DCG, January 1983.

[10] Ibid.

4

"I Married the Prettiest Girl in Town"

In June 1925, Greer was again working for contractor Homer Fry of Dallas, assigned to help develop the Park Highlands subdivision in Athens, building parks and golf courses. He continued to assist Fry as a landscape engineer on projects in Dallas.

One incident soon helped persuade the youthful Greer to look for another job.

"I was working over a yard in Dallas, when a fellow next-door called me to the fence and said he needed a yard-boy pretty bad. Was I available?"[1]

The next day, Greer heard the call for a new city engineer at Athens, and he drove down to apply.

Greer was hired by Athens, on condition that he would grow a mustache to look more mature, put on a hat — and quit wearing an Aggie belt buckle.[2]

"I took two suggestions. I never did grow a mustache.[3]

"They voted some bonds and wanted to pave some streets," Greer summed up his career with the City of Athens.

"I spent their money . . . paved some streets . . . married the prettiest girl in town . . . then went with the Texas Highway Department, where I've been ever since."

"The prettiest girl in town" was Helen Colton, a petite and beautiful brunette, the daughter of Grocer Frank Colton.

Charles F. Hawn, a classmate of Helen in public school, described her as "a favorite with everyone."

Both Helen and Dewitt attended the First Methodist Church, and they married there on June 21, 1928, eight months after he had joined the Texas Highway Department as assistant resident engineer at Athens.

Greer had resolved never to get married until he was earning two hundred dollars a month.

"I had to wait," he reported.

"I went with Helen two years. She taught kindergarten. Meeting her was easy. I was making two hundred dollars a month as city engineer. My Model A Ford roadster with the Texas Aggie sticker was parked at the city hall. I was the most eligible bachelor in town."

Greer claims five or six young women left candy for him on the seat of his roadster, including Helen.

Dewitt and Helen courted on the front porch of her parents' home. The romance lasted until Helen's death in Austin in 1977, leaving Dewitt, one daughter, Ann Colton Juul (wife of an Austin banker) and two grandsons, Dewitt and Craig Juul.

During many years of their life in Austin, Helen was ill, a condition which brought Greer and their daughter into a more binding father-daughter relationship than might otherwise have occurred. "Ann Colton," as Greer always called her, was quite attentive to her father.

Charles F. Hawn, later a Highway Commission member, literally knew Greer from his first day in Athens.

"My Dad, W. A. Hawn Sr., was mayor of Athens, when Dewitt was hired as City Engineer. . . . We had a town character named Sam who was kept up by many of us over the years. Sam was not nearly as dumb as some of us thought. When Dewitt drove into Athens for the first time, he stopped at Stirman's Drug Store, which was our hanging out place and where Sam spent most of his time.

"When Dewitt stepped out of his car, Sam met him and asked for a cigarette."[4]

Somewhat annoyed, Greer gave the stranger a cigarette, adding "Why don't you buy your cigarettes? That's how I get mine."

"Well," chirped the moocher, "I never buy a cigarette, and I'll bet I smoke two to your one."

Hawn also reported on a "womanless wedding," an amateur theatrical where Hawn played the groom and the smaller Greer portrayed the bride. It raised money for the church.

"Ours was something for the books," Hawn chuckled.

"Womanless weddings" were comedy events on amateur programs during the 1920s.

In the summer of 1925, a group of Henderson county citizens hired Greer and Jed Robinson, then a Texas A&M freshman, to survey a route from Athens to Cross Roads.

It was truly a moonlighting job. The surveyors worked at night, to save money and because they could have dates on the job with them. Robinson went several miles ahead of Greer, and fired skyrockets, which Greer watched through a transit. He took the average transit reading and ran the survey line on that bearing.

"There is no record of this method being used in roadbuilding either before or since," proclaimed the Texas Good Roads/Transportation newsletter of October 1981, crediting the story (which Greer confirmed) to Mary Hunter in the *Athens Daily Review*.

After graduation, Robinson became an engineer for the Highway Department, and retired in 1972 as construction engineer. He died at Athens in 1983.

In November 1927, Greer achieved his ambition to work for the Texas Highway Department. His first job was an "instrument man" laying out a highway system for Henderson County. The title: assistant resident engineer.

Then in 1929, Greer was named acting district engineer of the Tyler District, a position held for two years until he became district engineer.

A colleague claimed that Greer actually won the top position at Tyler because State Highway Engineer Gibb Gilchrist couldn't make up his mind which of two well-qualified more senior engineers in the district should get the appointment.[5]

While Gilchrist pondered for nearly two years, "Greer did such an outstanding job that Gilchrist had to keep him on."

One of Greer's problems in management was his youthful appearance. Some old-timers in the Tyler district called him "the Kid." According to one story, when the new district engineer appeared to inspect a culvert-pouring project, the contractor told him: "Move over, son, and let us get in here."[6]

The "youngster" quickly earned the respect and admiration of his colleagues in East Texas, as well as state headquarters in Austin.

"He had the human touch," recalled Jed Robinson, then an engineer at Tyler and later an official of the department in Austin. "He was interested in people. He got into all phases of operation for his own edification."

Greer's early experience with authority had its rough spots.

Once, District Engineer Greer ordered a man with a team of mules stationed on a muddy place in the road to pull vehicles to more solid ground, where they wouldn't "get stuck" as early motorists often did in wet weather.[7]

The foreman directing traffic across this mudhole, an officious type, was told one motorist at the back of the line was Cone Johnson, Tyler lawyer and member of the Texas Highway Commission.

The foreman directed "Mr. Johnson" to the head of the line and moved his car through the mud while other motorists waited.

It turned out later "Mr. Johnson" was just a fast-talking snuff salesman. The foreman became furious when he learned he had been tricked.

Later, District Engineer Greer arrived at the mudhole in his Reo car marked "State Highway Department," drove up to the barricade and asked permission to drive through to inspect construction work ahead.

The flagman told him to wait.

"You don't seem to understand. I'm the district engineer and I must inspect the job," said Greer, certain that the man must have noticed his state-marked, mud-spattered Reo.

"I don't care if you are Jesus Christ, you can't go in there," retorted the flagman. "I let a man in yesterday who said he was Cone Johnson and the foreman almost fired me."

Greer pointed to the forest bordering the muddy road, and asked the flagman if he could see the fire in the distance. While the man was searching the woods, Greer drove through the barricade, and on his way.

The Cone Johnson referred to above, and State Highway Engineer Gilchrist were two great influences on Greer's life and career.

Lawyer Johnson was a close friend of Dewitt's father, Sam Greer, and was a lifelong booster of his family.

"We used to sit on the (Smith County) courthouse lawn in Tyler and talk highways," Dewitt Greer said of his friendship with Highway Commissioner Johnson. Through him, it was easy to know Gilchrist."[8]

Greer spoke reverently of Gilchrist, who gave the young engineer his start.

"Gibb Gilchrist was probably the guiding light of my life."

". . . Gilchrist is the man who set the pattern of honesty, integrity and hard work that molded the department.[9]

"Gilchrist was tough, but he was the best man to handle the transition from corrupt politics. He made the way easy for the rest of us."

The seven years in Tyler were good ones for the Dewitt Greers. The operation of the District Office under Greer attracted favorable attention in Austin and elsewhere.

State Engineer Gilchrist brought Dewitt to Austin as one of the department's youngest division heads in history. Even so, the family's departure was delayed until after the birth of the Greer's daughter, Ann Colton, in Tyler in 1935.

Ceremonies praising Greer's services were held all over the Tyler district before his departure.

Smith County Judge Brady P. Gentry, later instrumental as State Highway Commission chairman in promoting Greer to head the state department, told Tyler Rotary Club members that under Greer's leadership the Tyler Highway District had come to rank in excellence with the larger districts at Dallas and Houston.[10]

"Dewitt Greer is practical," praised Judge Gentry. "He knows his job and does it well. He doesn't try to take credit for what he doesn't do.

"He stands as high as any man could with the county commissioners' courts in this district, although at times he has had to refuse some of the requests of the various courts. All of the commissioners' courts respect him and have confidence in him."

At the time, commissioners' courts loomed larger in highways construction and maintenance than they did later after the state and federal governments took over the expensive task of building a truly statewide and then an interstate system. The confidence of the county officials in state highway authority was very important.

Greer expressed regret at leaving his beloved East Texas.

"I hate to leave Tyler and East Texas," he told his fellow-Rotarians. "But I'm not leaving for good. I'm going to Austin where I hope to do the most good for East Texas.''[11]

Credit for the recognized success of the highway construction and maintenance program in the Tyler district went to Greer's co-workers.

''. . . This division stands out over any division in the state, and none of the credit should go to me,'' said Greer. ''The reason this district stands out is because of the fine, efficient personnel, and the credit should go to those men who have done the work — even to the man with the shovel.''

Dewitt Greer became a team player from the outset of his career, and never hesitated to share credit with fellow-workers.

The Rotary Club's farewell resolution to Greer on November, 19, 1936, thanked the departing district engineer for serving ''unselfishly, patriotically and diplomatically . . . without fear, favor or political regard . . .''[12]

While Dewitt Greer never aspired to elective office, his manner, knowledge, and diplomacy made him one of the most effective persuaders in the history of state government. He developed skill at telling pompous elected officials ''No'' and making them like it. They often went away converted to Greer's way of thinking.

So eager was Greer to accept a promotion to the state headquarters that he took a cut in salary, from $408 per month as district engineer to $333.33 as chief engineer, construction and design.

L. H. Davis of Tyler wrote this farewell poem to express how East Texans felt about their departing engineer:

TO THE TUNE OF "SMILES"

There are roads that make us dizzy,
There are roads that make us sore
There were roads like this in old Smith County
But it's hard to find them any more.
There are roads that curve and have a leaning,
That in daylight only we can see.
But the roads that keep us from careening,
Are the roads that you built for me.[13]

[1] *Austin American-Statesman*, Charles E. Green, 1940.

[2] Ibid.

[3] Greer interview, January 1983.

[4] Letter from Hawn to the author, Aug. 29, 1983, and from transcript of the Highway Commission honoring Greer on his 35th anniversary with the department, July 31, 1962.

[5] Golden Anniversary history, p. 37.

[6] Ibid.

[7] Ibid., p. 38.

[8] Interview with DCG, May 4, 1983.

[9] Golden Anniversary history, p. 39.

[10] *Tyler Morning Telegraph*, 1936.

[11] Ibid.

[12] State Highway Department files.

[13] "Our Curious Times" column, Chauncey Speer, *Tyler Daily Courier-Times*, date unknown.

5

A Foundation Is Built

The ten years before Dewitt Greer joined the Texas
Highway Department as assistant resident engineer at
Athens had been turbulent.

Gibb Gilchrist was a central figure, and his main ad-
versaries were the Governors Ferguson and many members of rural county commissioners' courts jealous of authority over roads and financing, plus like-minded members of the Texas Legislature.

Under Gilchrist, as Dewitt Greer recognized early,
the Texas Highway Department entered upon a course
of excellence and integrity. Greer built on that base, adding important contributions of his own.

Born in 1887 at Wills Point, in northeast Texas, Gilchrist, like Greer, learned early the difficulty of moving
on muddy roads and over the dusty, rough terrain of the
few dirt roads even in dry weather.

Although his real first name was "Gibb," some official records show "Gilbert Houston Gilchrist," which he
chose to satisfy the registrar at the University of Texas
at Austin.[1]

Gilchrist received a civil engineering degree at the university in 1909, worked for several years for the Santa Fe Railroad, became a captain in the Corps of Engineers in World War I, and then joined the fledgling Texas Highway Department in southwest Texas. By 1924, Gilchrist was state highway engineer and was involved with "good roads" advocates in trying to settle the stormy and sometimes seamy affairs of the state agency.

His first stint as head of the department ended in resignation after a few months, caused by political differences with the Fergusons.

After two years as a consulting engineer in Dallas and the election of Dan Moody as governor, Gilchrist returned as state highway engineer in the new administration starting in January 1927. He remained until 1937 when Texas A&M offered Gilchrist, a state university graduate, the position of dean of engineering.

"I was surprised that Gibb took that job," Greer said years later of Gilchrist's final move.

Under Governor Moody, the Highway Commission and Department were quickly reorganized. Ross S. Sterling, a Houston oilman-banker and contributor to Moody's campaign, was named chairman of the commission. Cone Johnson, the Tyler lawyer, and District Judge Walter R. Ely of Abilene were appointed as new members.[2]

The new commission and Gilchrist quickly removed twenty-five top engineers in district and state-level positions — ending the Ferguson era of influence in the agency (although Mrs. Ferguson served another two-year term in 1933-1935).

By 1932, the Texas Legislature had given the department full control over the state highway system. The state assumed the bond obligations which counties issued early for local road-building. The state gasoline tax, set by lawmakers at one cent per gallon in 1923 to supplement funds from vehicle registration fees, had by 1932 been increased to four cents a gallon — three-fourths allocated to road building and maintenance and one-fourth to public education.

Federal funds, which had been allocated to states since a few years before the Texas Highway Department was created, gradually increased.

Before the 1930s, highways had been far from happy ways in the United States and Texas.

"Although the early Spanish explorers probably marked trails, the first definitely known roads in Texas were those opened in the early eighteenth century between Mexico and the missions of East Texas and at San Antonio and Goliad. Probably the first principal highway in Texas is that now known as 'The Old San Antonio Road.' Early Texans traveled a blazed trail known as 'Trammel's Trace.'

"During the days of the Republic of Texas and early statehood (Texas joined the United States in 1846), stagecoaches operated over primitive roads marked between the leading settlements. The Central National Road of the Republic of Texas was approved by an act of Congress (Texas Republic) on Feb. 4, 1844, and although it never played the role that Congress visualized, it was a way of entry for many immigrants into Texas from 1843 to the coming of the railroads.

"The old Military Road ran from Red River through Dallas, Waco and Houston. Too often most of the roads could be described as a 'mere collection of straggling wagon ruts.' In 1852, Houston projected a plank road to the Brazos, and twenty-three miles of the proposed route were graded. Toll roads were discussed but none was built."[3]

Just as "El Camino Real," the Old San Antonio Road, had brought immigrants and the Mexican Army into Texas before the Republic was established, the primitive roads helped the new state to supply material to other parts of the Confederacy in the War Between the States.

The post-Civil War period saw railroads spread much

faster than road transportation. Between 1870 and 1880, railroad mileage in Texas had increased from 711 miles to 3,293, but much of the vast state remained frontier territory.

"Acknowledging the state's inability to deal with the road problem," wrote Historian John David Huddleston, the Texas Legislature in 1879 authorized the counties to lay out, supervise, and maintain roads.

"The law also permitted the counties to draft the services of all males between eighteen and forty-five years of age to work on the roads for as many as ten days per year. Each man could either provide his labor, hire a substitute, or purchase an exemption at the rate of a dollar a day. Laborers worked under the watchful eye of the road overseer, but the greatest part of these efforts involved no more than clearing stumps and filling mudholes with dirt and rocks."[4]

Citizen labor was substituted for taxation, unless the citizen was willing and able to buy his way out of "working on the road."

Counties were permitted to levy property taxes for highway purposes later in the century, but still by 1900 "Texas roads bore no semblance to an integrated system."[5]

Highway expansion had come faster east of the Mississippi River than in Texas, but railroads and waterways remained the principal transportation until invention of the automobile. The population remained almost entirely rural. Most of the nation's paving was of cobblestones or wood blocks on downtown streets of New York, Philadelphia, and the few other cities of the Eastern Seaboard.

A Scotsman named John L. McAdam literally helped lay the foundation for highways of the future. About 1820, he developed the idea later adopted by American road-builders: instead of massive foundation courses of stone, McAdam built roads of native soils, topped with native rock, broken into small enough pieces to pass

through a two-inch ring. "Macadamized" building became the wave of the future for all-weather highway construction.[6]

In 1893, another great development came in the
form of the nation's first successful gasoline engine — invented by Frank Duryea, and tested in a modified coach
on the streets of Springfield, Mass.[7]

The next few years saw the Automobile Age burst
into the twentieth century, along with the birth of Dewitt C. Greer as one of its greatest builders of highways.

In 1908, Henry Ford of Detroit, Michigan, after ex-
perimenting with a heavier machine, designed his Model
T Ford automobile, which truly put America on wheels.
Ford also invented the industrial assembly line, which
enabled mass production of low-cost motor vehicles.
Forthwith came a public clamor for more and better
roads.

The first recorded automobile trip in Texas took
place in 1899 when Col. E. H. R. Green, an eccentric railroad tycoon traveled thirty miles from Terrell to Dallas
in five hours and ten minutes.

The *Dallas Morning News* reported that Green "created a sensation last night."[8]

"At 7:30 o'clock he rode up and down Main Street
(Dallas) in a horseless carriage at the rate of fifteen miles
per hour.

"Accompanied by a gentleman who is an expert in
handling these vehicles, Mr. Green left Terrell yesterday
at 2:20 o'clock for Dallas more than thirty miles away.

"Near Forney, they were crowded off the roadway
into a gully by a farm wagon. The water tank was dam-
aged so that it began to leak and a stop of half an hour
was necessary to make repairs.

"Mr. Green arrived in Dallas at 7:30 o'clock, having
made the trip in five hours and ten minutes."

Today, the trip can be made in half an hour over Interstate Highway 20, without much risk of being crowded
into a ditch by a farm wagon.

Colonel Green related his experience on the trip:[9]

"It was amusing to notice the sensation our appearance caused along the road. Cotton pickers dropped their sacks and ran wildly to the fence to see the strange sight. And the interest was shared by farm animals, too. One razorback sow that caught sight of us is running yet, I know.

"At least a dozen horses executed fancy waltz steps on their hind legs as we sped by and but for the fact we were soon out of sight, there would have been several first-class runaways.

"When we reached Dallas, however, the city horses, used to electric cars (streetcars) and other things alarming to most equines, did not even lift their heads.

"I have no idea of the speed of the vehicle. We did not put it on full power on the country roads because it would have been too dusty for comfort.

"When we reached the asphalt pavement of Main Street, we dared not drive fast because the thoroughfare was so crowded it would have been dangerous to human life."

Farmers with their horse- and mule-powered transport disliked the automobile, which raised clouds of dust and frightened the livestock. Further, the early roads attracted sports trying out their new machines.[10]

Farmers in one Grayson County community decided to stop maintaining the roads "for road hogs and speed cranks."

Although sparsely settled, West Texas roads concerned its people from the time Coronado staked the first highway across the great Plains in 1541.[11]

In the 1880s, a furrow was plowed across the plains from Amarillo to Roswell, New Mexico, with surveying and marking financed by Amarillo businessmen.

The first automobile appeared on Amarillo streets early in the twentieth century, a one-cylinder Cadillac driven by a Dr. Lockett. By 1910, the town had over two hundred motor vehicles. Many years passed, however, before a motorist from Amarillo could drive to Dallas-Fort Worth over an all-weather highway.

But the Golden Age of the Automobile was under way, aided by oil discoveries in Texas to furnish the gasoline.

[1] *Handbook of Texas*, Vol. III, p. 338.
[2] "Good Roads for Texas," Huddleston, pp. 85-86.
[3] *Handbook of Texas*, Vol. I, p. 810.
[4] "Good Roads for Texas," Huddleston, p. 24.
[5] Ibid., p. 25.
[6] American Public Works Association, *History of Public Works in the United States, 1776-1976*, p. 59.
[7] Ibid., p. 73.
[8] Golden Anniversary history, p. 10.
[9] Ibid., p. 10.
[10] Ibid.
[11] L. P. (Pete) Gilvin of Amarillo, April 1975, addressing West Texas Highway Association in Brownwood.

6

Rise to the Top

State highway authority and skilled manpower were in place when Dewitt Greer moved to Austin in 1936. Funds, however, were relatively scarce until World War II ended in 1945, when Greer directed the greatest program of highway construction the world ever witnessed.

In 1936 when Greer took over as chief engineer, construction and design, for the Highway Department, politics still threatened the agency's operation although Gibb Gilchrist was clearly the man in charge, but answerable to the three-member Highway Commission appointed by the governor.

Gilchrist surprised Greer and many others by resigning as state highway engineer in September 1937 to become dean of engineering at Texas A&M.

Gilchrist wrote Greer, before leaving, commending the young East Texan.

"I remember about thirteen years ago, your father wrote me a rather insistent letter, to the effect that the State of Texas was losing something by not having you in our service," said Gilchrist. "I was impressed by the letter to the extent I remember it yet, although I haven't seen it for thirteen years.[1]

"I remember when you held a minor office in the (Tyler) Division and I made no mistake in advancing you to district engineer. Your work at Tyler, during the oil boom particularly, was outstanding." (The world's largest oil field at the time was discovered in the Tyler District in October 1930, and became the scene of feverish development.)

Gilchrist continued:

"Your work here in Austin has been outstanding and will continue to be so if you are permitted to operate. . . . In no case have you ever been a disappointment but have measured up far beyond the average expectancy, and it has been much to my pleasure. I hope that the future will hold much for you. It should. . . ."

In addition to fighting for non-political management of highway building and maintenance in Texas, Gilchrist's final service in nearly ten years as department head saw these significant changes:

In 1929, the state gasoline tax for financing highways was increased to four cents a gallon (from two cents). The State Highway Patrol was established, as part of the Highway Department. (The Department of Public Safety was established six years later and took over highway policing.)[2]

In 1932, county financing of state highways was ended, except for right-of-way, and the Legislature passed the State Assumption Law to pay off previously issued county road bonds through allocation of one cent from the state gasoline tax. The Highway Department's district offices were increased to twenty-five.

In 1933, the state headquarters moved into the attractive State Highway Building (Later renamed the Dewitt C. Greer Building), across Eleventh Street south of the State Capitol in Austin.

In 1936, thirteen tourist information centers were established on the state's border at highway points with the greatest interstate traffic.

Highway beautification also originated under Gilchrist. In 1933, Jac L. Gubbels, former landscape engineer for the City of Austin, was employed as the State Highway Department's first landscape architect, financed partly with federal funds.

Under Gubbels' supervision, thousands of trees were planted and tons of wildflower seed spread along rights-of-way.

Highway employees, Boy Scouts, and school children participated in the program, which planted redbud, dogwood, crepe myrtle, native oaks, agarita, and numerous other native trees and shrubs along highways all over Texas.

Six years later in 1939, a Texas Highway Department report commented:

"Federal aid funds have been used for landscape work in planting 40,000 trees, 315,000 shrubs, vines and perennials on 482 miles of highway and improving 20 intersections. In addition, state maintenance forces have planted over 400,000 trees and 698,000 shrubs. An estimated eighty tons of wildflower seeds, threshed and unthreshed, have been collected by Boy Scouts, school children, and highway employees for sowing along the highways."[3]

The Fergusons made one more attempt to impose their influence directly into highway affairs during the Gilchrist administration.

Elected for a second and final term in 1932 over incumbent Governor Sterling, Mrs. Ferguson named a friendly highway contractor, Frank L. Denison, the beneficiary of Ferguson favors in previous years, to the Highway Commission. Senators rejected the appointment, and Attorney General James V. Allred acted to stop the appointee from attempting to sit with the commission anyway.

Next, the Fergusons tried to get legislative approval of changing the Highway Commission from three appointive members to five elective members, with provi-

sion for Mrs. Ferguson to name an interim commission if
voters approved the new system. The recommendation
failed in the Legislature.[4]

The Senate confirmed Mrs. Ferguson's choice of John
Wood of Center to the Highway Commission. While re-
maining friendly to the Fergusons, Wood cooperated with
the commission majority in following the course set by
Gilchrist and the commissioners appointed by Governors
Moody and Sterling.

Gilchrist survived the Fergusons' final sortie into
highway affairs, but his political troubles persisted with
the election of Jimmy Allred, the former attorney general, as governor in 1934.

The uncertainty of dealing with Allred appointees on
the commission helped trigger Gilchrist's departure to
the deanship at Aggieland in 1937.

The *Dallas Morning News* editorially praised Gilchrist's decade at the helm:

"Public service is not always efficient service," the
newspaper said. "In general it is well below the level of
performance that private industry has been able to command and get. But when public service calls to itself men
who maintain high ideals and who give their best endeavors, it is always able to hold its own against any field of
endeavor."

Texas had been fortunate to have a man of such
character and attainment during the Highway Department's decade of leadership under Gilchrist, the editorial
added.

Historian Huddleston evaluated the next three
years as follows:[5]

"The Allred-controlled road commission named Julian Montgomery, a Lower Rio Grande Valley reclama-
tion engineer originally from Fort Worth, to succeed Gilchrist. It would have been virtually impossible for any
man to supersede Gilchrist's influence within the road
agency, and Montgomery — perceived as a yes-man — ran
into firm opposition on the part of many department

heads and district engineers. After three years, Montgomery resigned."

Gilchrist's departure and the unsettled conditions of the department, followed by Montgomery's resignation during Gov. W. Lee O'Daniel's administration, set the stage for the rise of Dewitt Greer to state highway engineer for Texas, a position he held for twenty-seven historic and eventful years.

The department and Texas citizens saw mostly hard years during the time that Gilchrist and his supporters were laying the foundations on which his successors were to build.

The Great Depression struck in 1929, hitting the state treasury and the road construction industry very hard. In 1933, Gilchrist wrote Highway Department heads urging tactful treatment of the many unemployed who sought work, any kind of work, but the openings were few. State employees were paid with treasury warrants which were discounted up to five per cent if cashed immediately.

Nevertheless, millions of automobiles, trucks, and buses were beginning to move over the roads of Texas, although many remained unpaved.

When the Texas Legislature passed the state's Drivers License Law in 1935, three million applicants received legal authority to operate motor vehicles. The first law required only a mailing fee and without any examination for a driver to become licensed. This writer, for example, received one of the original licenses and has renewed it through the years, with only an eyesight examination in later years required to qualify. New drivers were required later to pass examinations on vehicle operation and traffic regulations.

Despite the minimal license requirements in 1935, many Texans considered it an infringement on their independence and refused to obtain licenses, an attitude which diminished over the years but never disappeared entirely.

The first year of Governor Allred's administration (1935) also saw the creation of a separate Department of Public Safety, with its own governing board and administrator fashioned after the structure, which was proving effective for the Texas Highway Department.

The year 1936 marked the centennial of the Texas Republic, and the event brought thousands of tourists to Texas, especially for celebrations in Fort Worth and Dallas, whose shows attracted national attention. The Highway Department established the first information booths along the main entrances to the state to tell the visitors about the state's attractions.

The state and communities erected many permanent memorials to the men, women, and places which figured prominently in Texas history.

In October 1939, the Greer family and friends were saddened by the tragic death of Dewitt's mother in a West Texas traffic accident involving a drunk driver.

The Marvin Missionary Society of the Methodist Church in Tyler, eulogized her:[6]

"Mary Lou Greer brought out of life a determination which found happiness in unselfish service . . . in unforgettable love."

Her husband, Sam R. Greer, by then had built the Peoples National Bank into Tyler's largest.

[1] Letter to Greer from Gilchrist, THD files, Sept. 18, 1937.

[2] History and Present Status, State Department of Highways and Public Transportation, September 1982, pp. 32-33.

[3] "Good Roads for Texas," Huddleston, p. 205.

[4] Ibid., p. 187.

[5] Ibid., p. 202.

[6] Greer files.

7

State Highway Engineer Greer

While Dewitt Greer nurtured ambitions to head the Highway Department, he was surprised when in 1940 the offer came. Greer was only thirty-seven years old, very young for such a prestigious position in those days. Some older department heads and district engineers had never accepted Julian Montgomery during his three years at the helm after Gilchrist resigned.

Despite criticism from senior department employees, Montgomery is credited with emphasizing one policy which Greer continued in the department: giving credit to employees "in the ranks" for good performance.

The youthful division head — who looked even younger — was summoned to appear before the Highway Commission on July 1, 1940, and he did not know what to expect.

"I had no idea that I would be named state highway engineer that day," Greer recalled.[1] "The commission called me in and told me I was 'it.' I don't know exactly why they picked me, although I did have a good background of design and construction and had worked at just about every phase of highway work."

Greer did have a personal friend on the commission. Brady Gentry of Tyler, a friend of the Greer family, had been named chairman of the Highway Commission in 1939 by Gov. W. Lee O'Daniel. Gentry's colleagues were Robert Lee Bobbitt of San Antonio and Harry Hines of Wichita Falls, both prominent in Texas politics.

Although the promotion was unexpected, Greer moved quickly to establish himself and his policies.

In November 1940, he called in the twenty-five district engineers for their first conference.

The occasion resembled a herd of old mules looking at a new gate.

One old-timer at the meeting remembered it as follows:

"There were some tough old district engineers in the group. They fought him (Greer) the first day, and they fought him on the second day. But before the meeting was over on the third day, there was no doubt in anybody's mind about who was the boss."[2]

Greer had gotten the group's attention, and he set out to gain their respect. He established the policies which marked his next twenty-seven years at the helm of the department.

"The first thing I did as state highway engineer was to go on an economy binge," Greer reported. "I thought there was a lot of money being wasted. It was my first crusade."

Years later, when this writer interviewed numerous people about Greer's career, I found lavish praise but little criticism. Pressed with a question about whether they found any faults with their long-time co-worker and friend, one replied:

"Well, Mr. Greer was a tightwad."

Said another: "Tight as paper on the wall."

Greer carried this rare quality for a public official into his private life. Although he spent billions of the taxpayers money, without any scandal, Greer always handled, the public's funds as carefully as his own, which is to say frugally.

It was a quality which associates came to learn early about the man.

Once, when Luther DeBerry, later head of the department, was put in charge of the hefty highway budget, Greer advised him:

"If you let the outgo exceed the income—out you go."[3]

Greer was as sparing with words as he was with funds.

When Greer promoted DeBerry from assistant engineer of the San Antonio district to the district engineer at Lufkin, DeBerry asked if Greer had any advice for him.

"You know enough after all these years (then twenty-five years with the department). That's all you need."

The onset of U.S. involvement in World War II in December 1941 upset Greer's drive for economy. The nation's main thrust became winning the war rather than limiting the expense.

"About the time I was getting more miles for the money, World War II hit. After the war, it was a matter of expeditious extravagance," Greer explained.[4]

"From time to time, I've gone on economy crusades. There were two things that I have emphasized during my twenty-seven years. Those are economy and decentralization. If we are not careful, department procedures become centralized in Austin. Only policy guidance must come from Austin. We must keep the initiative in the field."

Greer has referred to the districts as "the twenty-five highway departments of Texas."

District engineers under Greer enjoyed great autonomy but were held strictly accountable for their own conduct and that of their staffs. One long-time district engineer, friend of Greer's, was dismissed over a conflict of interest involving an investment by the engineer's wife which was against department policy.

To Greer, the reputation of the Highway Department and its people was paramount.

One superior who had treated Greer unfairly as a new highway employee never received rebuke or punishment after Greer reached a position of authority over the man's career. The employee was deemed to be doing a satisfactory job for the department.

Whereas Greer took a pay reduction when he moved up from district engineer at Tyler to head of the Construction and Design Division in Austin, he received a raise with the promotion to state highway engineer in 1940.

His new salary was $645 a month, $7,750 per year, and it remained at that level through World War II. New secretaries drew higher pay than this when Greer retired as chairman of the Texas Highways and Motor Transportation Commission August 31, 1981.

When Greer became state highway engineer, the Texas highways system totaled 22,207 miles. When he retired forty-one years later, the system totaled 72,945 miles — ample proof that the dedicated East Texan was indeed King of the Road Builders.

Growth had proceeded at a relative snail's pace in the department's early years, beset by lack of funds, political problems, and jealousy among county, state and federal officials over who would administer the spending which seemed certain to accompany expansion of public roads made necessary by the massive output of private motor vehicles.

Perhaps the most welcome endorsement which the new state highway engineer received came from Gibb Gilchrist.

Handwritten and addressed to "Dear Dewitt, Helen and Ann C. (the daughter)," Gilchrist wrote, as he commented, "really from my heart."[5]

"The State of Texas is fortunate in having you, Dewitt, at the head of its Highway Department which, you must know, I sincerely and unselfishly love.

". . . You are the head of the greatest organization in the country. You are fully qualified to be the head of it. I predict your administration will be outstanding in every way because you have the training, the temperament, courage and ability, just what is needed.

"I am not going to offer any advice to you — you remember the old saying 'Deliver me from my friends — I can take care of my enemies.' You know I am at your service at any time I might be able to render you and the state any service.

"And for you, Helen, no small part of Dewitt's success may be laid at your door. You can and will be of much aid to him in his greatly enlarged responsibilities. You will be greatly exasperated as the sham and hypocrisy of certain elements of human nature stand revealed, but these things will be greatly over-balanced by the bright and good side even though it takes its toll of home life. . . ."

Gilchrist closed with word that friends at "the College" (Texas A&M) wanted to honor the new state officials with a small dinner to be attended also by Thomas H. MacDonald, director of the U.S. Bureau of Public Roads and later on the A&M highway research staff.

Such heady recognition from Gilchrist, who had already distinguished himself in the highway world made Greer even more certain that he had made the right choice when he came to Austin from his better-paying job at Tyler, and that he again later made the correct decision when he passed up an opportunity to become head of the highway department for the State of Arkansas.

Soon after Greer came to Austin, he was contacted by Tucker Royall, an East Texas banker, who had been asked by J. H. Alpin, chairman of the Arkansas Highway Commission, to see if he could persuade Greer to head that state's highway department at a salary of $6,500 a year, about $2,000 more than Greer was making at the time.[6]

Greer considered the opportunity seriously, but declined.

"I am still of the opinion that in spite of the attractive features of your proposition, Texas offers me the best opportunities in my chosen profession," Greer replied.

The imminence of war blunted Greer's ambition to construct a first-class highway system for Texas at low cost. While the United States was not yet into the fray, its preparedness efforts increased rapidly, which brought much greater military training facilities in Texas.

Federal defense officials designated 6,375 miles of Texas highways, nearly one-third of the entire system and more than any other state, as being of strategic military importance.[7]

But extensive army maneuvers in 1940 revealed only one-fourth of the East Texas roads used met federal military standards, and hundreds of miles of roads and many bridges suffered damage from the heavy traffic.

When Pearl Harbor was attacked by the Japanese, Dec. 7, 1941, State Highway Engineer Greer offered to send whole construction units to the military but the offer was rejected by federal authorities on the ground such workmen were needed more for the states to build and maintain the necessary highways, air-strips, and other facilities which the war effort required—in a hurry.

Many department employees joined the military, however, and Greer himself tried to join the Navy in 1942, but was turned down as being too essential in his state position.

Besides being a former member of the Texas A&M military corps, with dozens of friends and classmates in the service, Greer had a personal reason for wanting to do more than his share in World War II.

His younger brother, Sidney Robert Greer, another Texas Aggie, was a captain of engineers at Corregidor in the Philippines when the Japanese attacked there simultaneously with the disastrous raid on Pearl Harbor, Hawaii. Captain Greer was captured in 1942 and taken to Japan, where he died in a prison camp, Feb. 10, 1945, at the age of thirty.

Robert's death affected Dewitt Greer deeply. He blamed his brother's death on neglect and mistreatment by the Japanese, rather than combat.

In later years, many foreign countries sent representatives to observe Texas' highway development. Greer was unfailingly courteous and helpful to all except the Japanese, an associate reported. He couldn't bring himself to forgive the war-time enemy completely.

Although Dewitt never succeeded in getting into the uniform during the war, he received a special commendation from the Eighth U.S. Naval District in Dallas for recruiting more men than anyone else in Texas for the famed Seabees, Navy Construction Battalions.[8]

It announced that 108 men and 18 officers had been recruited for the Seabees from Greer's department, partly in response to a letter Greer sent all employees telling how greatly their construction skills were needed by the navy.

The navy noted that 900 Highway Department employees had volunteered for various branches of the service, and that recruiting flags flew over all twenty-five district offices of the Texas Highway Department.

"With them, as they turned in resignations and left the department, went not only Greer's good wishes, but the explicit promise that when they returned a job paying an equal or better salary would be ready," the navy noted.

Greer added: "We are operating now with 32 percent less men than before Pearl Harbor, but I'm not trying to hold them back. I'm trying to get them where they can be of the most help."

Gen. Richard Donovan, commander of the Eighth Corps Area at San Antonio, finally asked Greer to quit trying to send the Texas Highway Department personnel to war. He thanked Greer for the effort, but said the war effort needed Greer and the Highway Department for work in Texas. The general sent copies to other military units.

"That squashed any other efforts I might have made," Greer commented later.[9]

Strangely, another Dewitt Greer — unknown to the state highway engineer and without any evident kinship — received national publicity soon after World War II for invention in radio-teletype communication.

The other Dewitt Greer, a lieutenant colonel who had enlisted in the army at age seventeen, developed equipment which President Harry S Truman used to keep in touch with cabinet members and other government officials wherever the president traveled in the world.[10]

Although Colonel Greer grew up at Quitman, another East Texas town, the two men never met. Several friends of Dewitt of the Highway Department sent him clippings of Colonel Greer's achievements.

[1] Golden Anniversary history, THD, p. 38.
[2] Ibid.
[3] DeBerry interview with author, 1983.
[4] Golden Anniversary history, p. 39.
[5] THMTD files, dated July 8, 1940.
[6] Greer files, dated July 7, 1937.
[7] "Good Roads for Texas," Huddleston, p. 226.
[8] THMTD files, date unknown.
[9] Golden Anniversary history, p. 39.
[10] *Dallas Times-Herald*, Oct. 28, 1945.

8

"Put the Money Under the Rubber"

Dewitt Greer spent the first forty years of his life preparing to be the world's greatest highway builder and the next forty years fulfilling his dream.

World War II greatly restricted non-military construction of all kinds, because of shortages of labor and material. But Greer correctly perceived that the American love affair with motor cars was reaching such passionate proportions that more and better roadways, and more vehicles, would be the rage after the fighting ended.

During the war, while helping build military roads and facilities, Greer's department held together and made plans for the future.

Money which normally would have gone into road construction was invested in short-term government bonds, ready to put into postwar projects.

Starting in early 1943, Texas led the nation in planning for a massive expansion of the highway system after the war.

Brady Gentry, the Texas Highway Commission chairman, served as chairman of the American Association of State Highway Officials in 1943, and presented in Washington that group's plea for post-war highway planning to be followed by construction with federal aid.

Greer held a meeting of district engineers and department heads, laying out a $250,000,000 postwar building program in Texas. In January 1944, "good roads" advocates from Texas went to Washington to urge allocation of funds for a nationwide program.

Speaking to a U.S. Senate committee, Greer estimated it would take three-fourths of a billion dollars to meet Texas road needs in the immediate postwar period. A national inter-regional program, later the interstate highway system would include 2,725 miles within Texas, and cost an estimated $311,000,000. The system was built in decades after the war, but inflation added greatly to the eventual outlay.

Congress passed a $1.7 billion, highway construction bill in 1944, to be matched by the states.

Thanks to the foresight of Greer, the Texas Highway Commission and Department, Texas was far out in front with plans and matching money when the postwar construction deluge came.

The state's and nation's leaders laid out a three-level program of highway construction:

> The interstate system.
> The trunk line arterial system.
> Secondary and feeder roads, such as farm-to-
> market.

Greer later called the Federal-Aid Highway Act of 1944 a demonstration of "wise and courageous leadership in this country by forming a new approach to the problem of highway development. It is now accepted that this far-reaching legislation established the principle of a balanced system or pattern of development through the years that were to come following the close of the war."[1]

Few persons realized then, or now, how vast is the Texas system of roads and streets.

In 1944, Greer estimated the total at 196,000 miles, only 26,000 miles of which was paved.[2]

"With approximately 40 percent of the people of Texas making their living from the soil — compared with 22 percent in the average state — it is evident that a large proportion of our six million people must go back and forth on highways in order to earn their livelihood, and consequently, transportation is of much more importance to the future prosperity of Texas than it is to most of the other states. Yet we have barely scratched the surface in providing highway transportation for Texas...," Greer wrote.

From the first allocation of federal funds for postwar construction, Texas received $30,000,000 annually for three years, which included funds to build a sixty-mile road into Big Bend Park from Alpine.[3] The state first acquired the huge Big Bend area in 1941, but transferred it to the U.S. National Park System in 1944.

The day following approval in Congress of the federal aid postwar program in Washington, the *Austin American* commented editorially:

"TEXAS FORESIGHT
ON ROAD WORK
READY TO PAY OFF

"Windows of the Texas Highway Department building in Austin have been lighted up most of the nights for the past year and a half. State Highway Engineer Dewitt C. Greer and his staff have worked hours that would make proponents of a forty-hour week shudder.

"But now, those long hours and that arduous work are ready to pay off for Texas.

"The federal government's postwar highway program assures a $30,000,000 federal aid program for Texas in each of the first three years after the war.

"Texas has accumulated a fine backlog of state highway money. The Highway Commission and Gov. Coke Stevenson recommended, and the Legislature approved, keeping it intact and not diverting this cash surplus to other purposes.

"But money alone, federal and state, isn't enough to make the needed highway program translate itself from need to accomplishment. There is a formidable amount of engineering done to determine what roads should be built and improved first, and what type construction should be provided. Then, a truly gigantic task existed of preparing detailed maps, drawings, plans, and specifications to enable the work to be started.[4]

"That's what the night work, plus steady day work, was getting ready."

The gospel according to Dewitt Greer — "Put the Money Under the Rubber" — was about to be road-tested. The results were gratifying.

Greer held deeply the conviction that roads should be built where people would use them the most, and that income from the tax on gasoline, tires, and other costs of the journey would pay for the road. Travel generated construction and maintenance funds in proportion to the use, according to this formula.

While some deviation from the philosophy occurred over the years, Greer and other supporters of a first-class highway system for Texas generally fought successfully for spending "road user" taxes on highway improvement. Patently, it is as fair a tax system as man ever devised — let the user pay for the facility.

The principal deviation from this philosophy in Texas has been diversion of one-fourth of the motor fuel tax to support public schools, which political necessity brought about. It might be argued that school traffic pays a share also, at least on gasoline used to transport children and teachers.

Greer visualized the postwar highway building program, as a synchronized system of construction and re-construction.

". . . First take the secondary or feeder roads as provided in the (federal) act and note the traffic pattern as these roads are completed and placed under the wheels of traffic," he said.

"The farmer, the rancher, or simply the rural resident who had, in prior years, found it most difficult even to reach the nearest community with his motor vehicle, suddenly finds it is possible for him to move over a paved secondary road in all kinds of weather, not only to his nearest trading point but also to the far reaches of the trunk line highway system of this country. It would naturally follow then that this rural traffic begins to flow in all types of weather . . . and eventually reaches the urban and metropolitan centers of this country . . . forming a mass movement into the heart of these urban areas."[5]

For better or worse, the new farm-to-city all-weather system quickly changed the demographics of Texas and elsewhere. The departure of families from farms and small towns to the big cities accelerated after World War II and only in the 1980s were there signs that some residents of Texas' bulging cities preferred the quieter, simpler life of the countryside. The same roads which brought them to the metropolis often took them away, either for weekends or in some cases to rejuvenate the small towns within easy driving distance of the big-city attractions.

Texas built a unique financial base along with the best highway system in the world.

In 1945, voters adopted an amendment to the state constitution prohibiting the state government from spending money until the revenue was in hand or in sight — the so-called anti-deficit amendment. During the 1930s, the state assumed the bonded indebtedness which counties incurred earlier to build roads that became part of the state system. These bonds were repaid with state funds. But Texas never borrowed any money to build highways, while some other states were incurring debts which sometimes lasted longer than the roads they financed.

Not until 1955 did the Legislature see fit to increase the gasoline tax from four cents to five cents a gallon, still among the lowest in the nation. Later, the federal government began taxing gasoline and without the restraint which Texas had practiced voluntarily. As of 1983, Uncle Sam's tax totaled nine cents a gallon.

Cities and counties of Texas continued to borrow through bond issues for building roads and streets.

Economy-minded Greer viewed with some alarm when the eight years after World War II saw Texas cities increase their new bonded indebtedness by 850 percent compared with 1941, and street construction by 804 percent. The construction program, he said, sought to avoid "a catastrophe of traffic strangulation" from the explosion of city populations and vehicle traffic after the war.

During the same eight years, state highway construction increased by 185 percent, compared with the last prewar year, and counties continued to issue bonds for non-state highways as they more than doubled this building program.

To help meet the new situation, the Texas Highway Department established urban project offices in Dallas, Fort Worth, Houston, and San Antonio immediately after the war to expedite urban expressway construction. The first project finished was the Gulf Freeway between Houston and Galveston in 1951.

A major boost for Texas highway improvement came in 1946 when voters adopted the so-called "Good Roads Amendment" to the state constitution by an impressive four-to-one majority. It guaranteed that motor fuel taxes, drivers' license fees, and automobile registration income would be allocated for road purposes, ending a long period in which some legislators tried repeatedly but unsuccessfully to divert this revenue to non-highway purposes.

The Texas Good Roads Association supported the proposal and campaigned hard for its adoption. State Sen. Allan Shivers of Port Arthur (later governor) and Rep. Neveille Colson of Navasota sponsored the legislation, aided by Gov. Coke Stevenson.

In 1949, Shivers moved up to the office of lieutenant governor and Mrs. Colson was in the Texas Senate. Rep.

Dolph Briscoe, Jr., of Uvalde (another future governor) made his legislative priority that year the enactment of a farm-to-market road program, financed by a special appropriation. Mrs. Colson sponsored the bill in the Senate and the Colson-Briscoe Act became another step forward in the long effort to get Texas citizens "out of the mud."

By mid-1947, less than two years following the surrender of Japanese forces marked the end of World War II, the Texas Highway Department had put more construction under contract than any state — indeed, had contracted one-fourth of all the work in progress in the United States.[6]

During the busy postwar period, Greer was strongly supported by his commission, the Legislature, and governors. Commission chairmen included John S. Redditt of Lufkin, Fred A. Wemple of Midland, E. H. Thornton, Jr., of Houston, Marshall Formby of Plainview, Herbert C. Petry, Jr., of Carrizo Springs, and Hal Woodward of Coleman.

Greer was receiving national accolades, including in 1963 the George S. Bartlett Award (American Association of State Highway Officials) as the nation's top highway administrator. Characteristically, Greer attributed the success of the Texas program to his staff and highway supporters.

Greer showed wit, wisdom, and political skills — as well as professional and administrative ability.

Twenty-two years after becoming Texas' highway chief, Greer quipped at an Austin civic club program honoring him that he "accepted this award with all the humility that a Texan can muster. . . ."

Then he quickly turned to introducing the Texas Highway Department's veterans as those who really deserved the plaudits for the Texas Highway Department's far-flung prestige.[7]

Governments of other states and foreign countries sent observers to learn how Texas was creating such a wonder in the highway world. In 1954, Greer toured

Western Europe, speaking on highway-building in several cities.

Dolph Briscoe became one of Greer's biggest boosters.

Recalling the 1949 legislative session when the young war veteran-rancher from Uvalde championed the cause of rural roads, Briscoe commented:[8]

"Dewitt knew better how to deal with members of the Legislature than anyone else that I have ever known.

"He knew that something was going to be done (in the 1949 legislative session) for rural roads and he wanted to see to it that it was done right, that the money was spent right, and that it would result in a uniform system of rural roads throughout the state.

"He knew, as did so many others, that in many cases the money going to the county would not be used for the construction of properly engineered roads and would not result in a uniform system. . . .''

Briscoe said Greer convinced Lieutenant Governor Shivers and Speaker Durwood Manford, along with other legislative leaders, that the farm-to-market road program should be administered by the State Highway Department so it would be well engineered and effficiently constructed.

"No one knew it publicly at the time but Dewitt Greer wrote the legislation," Briscoe continued. "Any one who reads that legislation carefully will be aware how skillfully it was written. Dewitt took no credit then for the legislation nor has he since but he is the man who deserves the full credit for it. With the leadership behind the legislation it easily passed."

The Colson-Briscoe Act assured Texans the finest farm road system anywhere. Greer called it "one of the most constructive pieces of legislation passed during my twenty-seven years as state highway engineer."

While Greer self-effacingly depicted himself as a public servant carrying out the wishes of elected officials and appointed governing members, everyone familiar with Greer knew he was being too modest.

This reporter watched many times as Greer addressed legislative committees and delegations appearing before the Highway Commission. Greer gave the impression that he was just there to be helpful; but in reality offered suggestions that usually wound up as the prevailing solution.

"(Greer) was the most effective public administrator that I have ever known," Briscoe described his long-time friend. "He had a knack for letting others take the credit for what he accomplished . . . members of the Highway Commission . . . governors . . . members of the Legislature. He always worked smoothly and effectively with each one."

Although his life was devoted to engineering and public administration, in this writer's opinion, Greer would have been equally successful as a legislator, governor, corporation president, or secretary of state. His skills with people were great and highly effective.

Greer's friends and admirers included the department employees with whom he worked and the contractors who built roads which the state planned, financed, and operated.

Clara Bewie, a fifty-year employee in the Highway Department's top echelon, said of her old boss:

"Mr. Greer had tact . . .. intelligence. He could turn you down in a nice way. . . . The only way you could tell when he was angry was when the back of his neck turned red. . . . You didn't feel like he was running the place — but he sure was."

Clara mentioned a younger woman who worked closely with Greer and the Highway Commission.

"She worshiped Mr. Greer. She couldn't decide whether Mr. Greer or Darrell Royal was God." The lady also was a University of Texas football fan, and Royal won national honors coaching there.

Greer once declared his greatest accomplishment was seeing persons whom he selected grow in their jobs.

"When I employ and promote the leaders of the

Highway Department and see them grow into the jobs,
then I have achieved a great degree of success. It is one
of the most inspiring and rewarding things about this
job."[9]

Favoritism played no part in the Greer system. Just
as he let a former superior, who had treated Greer badly
as a young employee, continue his career until retirement, so Greer's choice of people for promotion had
nothing to do with old school ties or personal friendship.

"I was an 'outsider' as a University of Texas graduate in a place full of Aggies, but it never counted against
me," said Luther DeBerry, whose forty-four years with
the department coincided with much of Greer's service.

"I never asked for a raise or promotion but got them
anyway,"[10] recounted DeBerry, who retired as Greer's
next-door neighbor in Austin. DeBerry's last seven years,
1973-80, were as engineer-director of the Texas Department of Highways and Public Transportation — a name
change ordered by the Legislature but disliked by most
old-time employees.

Greer refused to get involved with squabbles where
lower-ranked staff members had jurisdiction.

"If you get involved in the little things, then you
miss the big picture," Greer explained.[11]

The chief seldom requested anybody's resignation,
but followed a policy of complete trust in every employee
unless some cause for doubt arose, especially concerning
integrity.

One Greer management invention was "The One-
Rebuttal System."

If Greer issued an order with which a fellow-worker
disagreed, the boss gave him one rebuttal.

"Not only is it his privilege, but if he has objections,
I consider him derelict in his duty if he doesn't tell me,"
said Greer. "This is vital to any organization. I don't
want 'yes men.' But there is only one rebuttal. The responsibility was mine."

John Nations, a division head, agreed that Greer would "listen to the goofiest ideas" when running the department.

"You can disagree with him completely, and he doesn't hold it against you," Nations remarked. "He gives a little and he takes a little."

Once, when an employee was hospitalized with pneumonia, Greer sent condolences and advised the man to stay off the job until he got well.

"But come back with some new ideas," the chief added.

Greer was an idea merchant and he expected help from his top assistants.

Highways were central to his mind.

"Greer has lived his whole life for the Highway Department," said an old-time associate. "All he talks about is highway work. He does relax occasionally, but he's soon back to his favorite topic. If we were having coffee right now, that's what he would be talking about." [12]

Although frugal and direct, Greer was more considerate of his staff than of his own well-being. "Work is my hobby," he said. [13]

Two accomplishments toward the end of his service as state highway engineer were getting substantial salary raises for department employees and establishing a retirement system which was later expanded to include all state employees.

Fairness with contractors marked Greer's whole career, while he maintained an arm's length relationship with them and demanded the same of his staff.

While working for a private contractor in the 1920s, Greer noticed the state supervisor working demanded larger loads of gravel than the contract specified. By the time the contractor's complaint came up for hearing, Greer was working for the state.

Nevertheless, he made an affidavit that his old employer had been cheated, and the contractor received payment for the extra material.

Perhaps Greer's closest friend among private contractors was L. P. (Pete) Gilvin of Amarillo, who had
worked with Greer when the two were young men helping get East Texas "out of the mud."

Despite Greer's pleasant exterior and diplomacy,
Gilvin said "it took a hard-nosed guy to straighten out
the department" when Greer was appointed chief, July
1, 1940. Greer filled the role well.

But the state engineer deferred to district engineers
in the details of building highways and running their districts.

"Greer never had direct contact with the contractors
on these matters," said Gilvin. "He was all business.
Specifications can be interpreted differently, but the
best jobs we ever had were when state engineers helped
with our problems. They never gave us a damn thing."

"A good contractor is entitled to a good inspection."[14]

Gilvin declared every contractor he knew had "complete admiration" for Greer and the Texas Highway Department. "I never heard any criticism of the man."

This respect and honorable relationship paid off for
the taxpayers, too.

Greer wrote for the *Handbook of Texas Supplement*
in 1976:[15] "A key factor in the success of the highway
program in Texas has been the development of the private contracting industry. Texas highways are designed
and the construction is supervised by the Texas Highway Department. Actual construction is performed by
private contractors under a competitive bid system.
More than three hundred contractors regularly bid on
highway projects in Texas.

"Keen competition has caused development of better
equipment and more efficiency among road-builders.
These have made the extensive highway program in
Texas possible within a sound financial framework.

"Texas builds better highways more economically
than most other states. For example, the national average
cost of new interstate construction is about $1,200,000

per mile, compared to the average cost in Texas of $750,000 per mile."

While these decade-old figures began rising rapidly with inflation in the 1970s, the proportion continued to hold with Texans getting more than other states for "money put under the rubber."

Moreover, the Texas Highway Department under Greer's direction made such a fast start at the end of the war on getting thousands of miles of highways built quickly — because it had plans and matching money — that the total savings ran into many millions of dollars.

An example of the size of this effort came toward the end of Greer's twenty-seven-year tenure as state highway engineer. The two years ended in August 1966 saw the state alone contract and start construction on 22,338 miles of new highway — almost equal the state's whole paved highway system of twenty years earlier! [16]

[1] THPTD files.
[2] *Texas Progress* magazine, August 1944, p. 13.
[3] Associated Press, Nov. 11, 1944.
[4] Dec. 1, 1944.
[5] THPTD files, about 1953.
[6] "Good Roads for Texas," Huddleston, p. 235.
[7] *Dallas News*, Morehead, Sept. 15, 1963.
[8] Letter to the author, May 17, 1983.
[9] Golden Anniversary history, THD, p. 40.
[10] Interview with author, 1983.
[11] Golden Anniversary history, p. 40.
[12] Ibid., p. 41.
[13] Interview with the author, 1983.
[14] Interview with the author, 1983.
[15] Page 391.
[16] Ibid.

9

"There's Never Been
Anybody Like Him"

Maps have been a source of joy and despair to the Texas Highway Department, especially the state maps given free to motorists. The state spends $100,000 a year producing a million or so new maps, mostly given away to motorists.

When Gibb Gilchrist headed the department, he once drew a reprimand from the Senate for printing maps in color, an unthinkable extravagance at the time.

About 1950, the map omitted the location of Mineral Wells, the small city west of Fort Worth that once was a health resort depending heavily on tourists seeking relief from bodily ailments through drinking the town's laxative waters.

Much banter and some serious criticism followed the oversight, from individual newspapers, and the Mineral Wells Chamber of Commerce.

A handwritten letter from West Texas accused State Engineer Greer of deliberately leaving Mineral Wells off the map.

"I want to go see my girl-friend, Rosita, but with no Mineral Wells on the map, I cannot find her," the letter lamented.

Greer conducted an intelligence operation, since he had several friends capable of writing such a letter. He traced it to Midland, home of commission member Fred A. Wemple, Jr., a well-known practical joker.

The above account from Marshall Formby of Plainview, like Wemple, a former commissioner and chairman, illustrates that the men at the top mixed wit with business when dealing with Greer.

Greer could take it as well as hand it out.

Much joking concerned Greer's loyalty to Texas A&M, especially during football season. Greer was accused of paving every road leading to the Aggies' stadium at College Station.

The state engineer had an ally in meetings with the commission as long as Robert J. Potts served as commissioner (1949-55). Before the department was organized in 1917, Potts taught highway engineering at A&M, possibly the first such course offered in the United States.

When together with other commissioners, Greer and Potts often discussed happenings at "the College" as if A&M was the only institution of learning and football in the country.[1]

On or off the commission, Marshall Formby also kept up a repartee with Greer. After Greer retired in Austin and Formby's health also kept him close to home, Greer continued to receive odd notes from the high plains.

Typical was a card Greer received in 1982 signed "Jackie."

"Send money. I'm broke!" it pleaded.

Jackie Sherrill had just signed to coach the Texas A&M football team at a fabulous salary.

Greer knew instantly the card was Formby's work. Formby attended Texas Technological University and Baylor, rivals to the Aggies in the Southwest Conference.

The owner of an ancient rooming house once took the Highway Department to court in a dispute over how much would be paid for the structure, which stood in the way of a proposed expressway.

The owner insisted the building had a 120 percent occupancy rate.

"The matter went to court, because the Texas Highway Department simply could not believe that any dwelling could be occupied by more tenants than it had rooms," wrote Keith Elliott in a most delightful article about the puckish Greer.[2]

Recalling the dispute, which the department lost, Greer reported "we do now realize that a house can have more occupants than it has rooms.

"It turned out that the place was a bawdy house. Gentlemen, the Texas Highway Department now recognizes that a house is not necessarily a home."

Elliott explained that Greer knew how "to smite them with his abundant wit. He doubles their pleasure that way, for his humor is double-barreled. First, his wit is dry and razor-sharp, a perfect thing in itself. Second, it carries the impact of the unexpected. It surprises those who have only heard of Greer, a man of great dignity and a legend in his own time, that he is warmly human. . . ."

While department employees, except his oldest friends, always called the boss "Mr. Greer" even though they knew him long and well, the chief was more informal. A young lady named Bobby, for example, might hear Greer call her "Robert."

In his twenty-seven years as department head, serving with fifteen different commission members — three at a time — Greer never issued a two-signature order, which one member refused to sign. It was unanimous, or the decision waited. Although two commissioners can issue a valid order, if the third was hesitant or doubtful, the matter was carried over at least until the next meeting.[3]

"It is essential to have harmony among the commissioners," Greer said. "We must work as a team."

Greer kept vital information at his fingertips, although he considered delegation of authority to district and division heads the strength of the department.

Greer was called "the best bookkeeper the department ever had" although he never held the title.

"Hell, he keeps better books in his desk drawer than our accounting people do," declared one admiring colleague.

His days were orderly and busy.

Reviewing a typical day at the office in 1967, near the end of his service as administrator, Greer reported he started by reading and answering mail.

Each morning, Greer wrote terse memos on small pink cards which he attached to department papers reaching his desk. A "well done" note from DCG brightened the recipient's whole work. Others simply said "Do it," "See me," "O.K." or other unembellished comment.

The typical day mentioned above, after reviewing the mail and writing staff memos Greer:

Reviewed the docket for delegations to appear at the upcoming commission meeting, talked to three legislators and an official of the State Building Commission, telephoned a federal highway official in Washington about designation of national routes, signed more than fifty contracts, worked on the program for an upcoming American Association of State Highway Officials convention, discussed problems with a district engineer, read a report on truck traffic and loads, and tax income from diesel fuel."

A fast reader, Greer reached decisions quickly, once he knew the facts.

The man always seemed to have the upper hand.

"Greer is never on the defensive," remarked a longtime friend and colleague. "You may think you are attacking, but he always seems to have the ball. At least he can convince *you* he has the ball. . . .

"His image didn't happen by accident . . . He never

forgets anything . . . completely dedicated . . . hard work
and planning. . . ."

"Greer has had a tremendous impact on highways at
the federal level—and even the world, for that matter . . .
There's never been anybody like him."[4]

Greer had a remarkable memory, which served him
well throughout his career.[5]

"He received great loyalty from those associated
with him," said J. C. Dingwall, Greer's successor as
engineer-director in the department. Dingwall moved to
his old hometown of Comanche when he retired.

"Most of the day-to-day judgments and decisions in
the Highway Department were made by others (staff),
usually in the form of written recommendations, many
times more than one. He operated on a staff basis. Once
the recommendations were in and a judgment formed,
any dissenters were allowed one rebuttal. A decision
would then be made and the matter considered settled.
No more rebuttals or bickering. This was good administration and I followed the general pattern after he left
the department.

"He was a person of great patience but was tough
when it came time for disciplinary actions with personnel concerning honesty, integrity or misbehavior. He
was never tough on people making errors or honest mistakes."

Allan Shivers, the governor longest associated with
Greer (July 1949-January 1957) told the writer that the
combination of Gibb Gilchrist and Dewitt Greer directed
the Texas Highway Department into greatness.[6]

"Dewitt is a quiet fellow, and the fact that the Texas
Highway Department achieved such acclaim under his
quiet leadership is a tribute to his ability. He built on
what Gilchrist started, and Greer deserves credit for im-
plementing this fine program."

During the seven and a half years of Shivers' gover-
norship, the paved mileage of the Texas highway system
doubled.

Shivers also credited Greer with a "fine sense of detecting any impending scandal that might affect the department, and he dealt with it firmly. The department has a remarkable record for integrity."

Greer studied his lessons before entering a discussion. If uninformed on a subject, he would learn more about it before talking or acting.

The man hated controversy.

"If a commissioner had a question on an item in the agenda, it would be deferred so that the commission could be unanimous in its decisions," said Garrett Morris of Fort Worth, who served with Greer as a commission member.[7]

"Dewitt did not believe anything but trouble came from public discussion of problems (in the department), especially in the news media. All media coverage should be positive."

Despite his calm exterior, and diplomatic tact, Morris felt Greer "could be hard as nails" on occasion, especially dealing with opposition within the department.

Greer had his own system of defusing controversies facing the commission.

"My fondest memories of Dewitt Greer concern the way he handled the Highway Commission minutes (orders) each month," recalled Marshall Formby.[8]

"On a particular day in which we signed minutes and made so many decisions, Dewitt would meet with the three commissioners, and sometime J. C. Dingwall (assistant to Greer) would be with us. I would be with E. H. Thornton, Bob Potts, and later on Herb Petry and Charlie Hawn.

"Greer would enter the conference room with a basket full of minutes, reaching twelve inches high. As we sat there throughout the day, he would read to us what the minute did or did not do, and showed us he had signed it. Then he presented the minutes to us to sign. I can see him shuffling the minutes. Now Greer never really had any *bad* minutes, but he did have some that stunk a little and certainly some that were not as good as others.

"You could watch the expression on his face, when he turned to pick up the top minute and present it to us, if it were a "bad"minute, you could see Dewitt frown and he would slowly place the typed minute in the bottom of the basket. He would do this all during the day and by four o'clock all of his 'not so good' minutes would be at the bottom of the basket. He worked on the theory that by that hour the commissioners would be so tired, they would sign anything in order to get to the supper which Herb Petry usually planned for us."

Commission members had ways of getting even with Greer on his cat-and-mouse tactics.

A dispute arose over locating a new farm-to-market road in Bastrop County, for example. Some farmers wanted the paved road routed over an existing hump-backed bridge; while a rival group favored another location. The commission dispatched member Marshall Formby and Assistant State Highway Engineer Dingwall to inspect the proposed routes, and recommend a location.

"We made the honorable decision to build farm-to-market roads on both proposed routes," Formby reported.

"Greer never got over this. He moaned about it ever since."

Once the commission met in an East Texas theater, part of the town's "Highway Week" celebration. Rain poured down outside. More people sat on the stage than in the audience.

Chairman Petry made the principal speech, then remarked in an aside to Greer:

"You'd think some of our employees would have showed up."

"Who do you think those people are out there?" quipped Greer.

Then one of the sparse crowd, a man in coveralls, walked to the front and took away the microphone and loudspeaker system, mentioning it had been rented for one hour and he had another call for it.

"That topped both our jokes," Greer lamented.[9]

A family feeling pervaded commission meetings with top staff members. Several days each month went into such sessions, although these later were shortened. Greer dined with the commissioners, and highways were the main topics there also.

"Greer was not a big, fat man like some of his commissioners," Formby commented. "He didn't eat as much in one day as some of us ate in one meal, but what he ate turned into energy."

When the commission wasn't in Austin, Greer ordinarily ate lunch at the counter of a bus station behind the Highway Building, and later at a cafeteria several blocks away. Coffee breaks, which later became malted milk breaks, also were taken at the bus station, attended by staff members and sometimes other friends.

When Greer lunched with commission members, they took turns paying the check.

Once, on a day when it was Greer's turn, he attended the commission hearing, then asked to be excused to go home because he did not feel well.

"Well," quipped Commissioner Hal Woodward, "I knew Greer was tight, but I never thought he'd stoop to this."

During his final years on the commission, Greer occasionally lunched with Garrett Morris, the former commissioner who had become chairman of the new Public Utilities Commission of Texas. Greer's favorite spot, said Morris, was a barbecue stand in northwest Austin. Greer's favorite meal: barbecue and banana pudding. Greer also loved chocolate, anything chocolate. "I eat chocolate every day," he told this writer.

Greer never bothered others with his personal problems, for he was a very private person.

"Honesty was one of his greatest assets," said Formby. "When you have fifteen thousand employees working for you, and human nature being what it is, it is certain that some time or other, some fellow gets his hand in the cookie jar.

"Dewitt could smell dishonesty clear across Texas, and he never whitewashed, but let the heads roll if necessary. He kept the department honest, and it was never out of whack more than thirty minutes at a time," commented Formby.[10]

Formby added Greer was always "honest and fair" with commissioners, even while using his own methods of persuasion and avoiding arguments.

Garrett Morris noted that Greer was protective of the department's interest against outside influences, including legislators and other politicians.

Morris recalled a campaign in the Legislature and outside for the Texas department to purchase a patented reflective material for stop signs, which would cost millions of dollars. Greer rejected the proposal, calling it unnecessary for safety, and the department kept making its own traffic signs.

Once Governor Preston Smith, who appointed Greer to the Highway Commission after Greer's retirement as department head, sided with Lieutenant Governor Ben Barnes in an effort to employ private engineering firms (rather than department engineers).[11]

"Dewitt politely pointed out to them" at a meeting in the governor's office "and to the firm making the presentation that the potential for fraud was so great that it was completely out of the question."

Morris recalled an incident concerning the special S.O. (State Official) license plates, which certain elected officials can obtain for personal vehicles.

The Legislature once eliminated judges from receiving such plates, and Their Honors were highly displeased.

"Recognizing the opportunity for good relations with the bench, Dewitt quickly formed a committee headed by Herb Petry to sit down with (Chief Justice Joe Greenhill of the Texas Supreme Court) and work out an acceptable substitute. This developed separate distinctive plates for state judges," explained Morris.

Although Greer always considered a healthy, profit-earning construction industry vital to Texas' highway program, he kept arms-length in dealing even with contractors who were long-time friends.

"A contractor couldn't buy him a cup of coffee," an employee stated.[12]

After watching the Texas Highway Department under Greer's direction, former Governor Allan Shivers remarked at a Texas Good Roads Association meeting:

"In twenty-five years there has not been a breath of scandal in the department."

Praise poured upon Greer after putting his imprint across the Texas landscape.

"The Texas Highway Department is one agency with which I have very little contact — simply because it is run so efficiently and well, with never a word of criticism," said Governor John Connally at a ceremony swearing in Hal Woodward (later United States district judge) for a second term on the commission.[13]

The *Texas Parade* magazine compared Greer with the greatest builders of all time:

"Not since Cheops erected his great Pyramid in Egypt, perhaps, has so singular a monument as the Texas highway system been engineered to one man's dream.

"The Texas highway web today (1965) exceeds 66,000 miles. Its mileage is twice that of Russia and it serves about as many vehicles (then about six million). Just the farm-to-market highway system of Texas exceeds all of the state highways in all of New England."[14]

Greer certainly didn't start with a flash in 1940. For one thing, Gibb Gilchrist was considered the best in the business when he resigned to move to Texas A&M. Greer was young, slight of build (125 pounds and five feet ten), and relatively unknown.

One humbling experience came soon after Greer moved into the department's top office.

Seeking to become better known, Greer made himself available to speak at luncheon clubs and other events.

He went to Uvalde to address a service club, prepared to be the principal speaker. He was ready to let the folks know what he had in mind for the department and state.

The invited speaker felt a bit strange when he was charged at the door for his meal and directed to a table in the rear of the room. The program proceeded without mention of Greer, until time to adjourn when the presiding officer noticed the visitor.

"—He almost fell out of his chair," reported J. C. Dingwall, without judging whether Greer or the presiding officer was more surprised.[15]

[1] Letter from Formby to the author, Mar. 8, 1983.
[2] *Texas Parade*, September 1965.
[3] Golden Anniversary history, p. 40.
[4] *Handbook of Texas*, p. 42.
[5] Letter to the author, March 1983.
[6] Interview with the author, Aug. 1, 1983.
[7] Letter to the author, Feb. 1, 1983.
[8] Letter to the author, Mar. 8, 1983.
[9] Dingwall letter, March 1983.
[10] Letter to the author, Mar. 8, 1983.
[11] Letter to the author, Feb. 1, 1983.
[12] *Texas Parade*, September 1965, Keith Elliott.
[13] Ibid.
[14] Ibid.
[15] Letter to the author, March 1983.

The 1918 graduating class of Pittsburg, Texas, high school. Dewitt Greer is the smallest youth, second row. He was fifteen
years old.   — Greer family files

Greer was reared in this home on Rusk Street in Pittsburg.

— Highway Department photo

The Greers attended Pittsburg's First Methodist Church.

— Highway Department photo

At Texas A&M, Greer served in the military corps and played trombone in the Aggie band.

Greer, far left, played in the Aggie jazz orchestra.

After graduating from A&M, Greer spent one year as an engineer and foreman of a Texas Parks Board building crew near Boerne. His workmen were all "trusty" convicts. Greer never got paid for his work but called it "the most interesting year of my life." The woman is a wife visiting her convict-husband. The man in boots and big hat is a Texas Ranger who brought the crew to camp. Greer took the picture.

— Highway Department reproduction

Greer's tent-office quarters at the convict camp. The car is a model T Ford roadster which he owned.

— Photo reproduction by the Highway Department

After serving as city engineer at Athens, then joining the Texas Highway Department, Greer married "the prettiest girl in town," Helen Colton, in 1928.

— Greer files, 1952 photo

A rare picture of Greer at play. Taken about 1937 on a ranch near Kerrville where the Dewitt Greers, the Gibb Gilchrists, and other friends vacationed.

— Greer files

Dewitt C. Greer as district engineer at Tyler about 1930. This Reo car was "handed down" from Commissioner Cone Johnson. Note cars had "running board" steps.

— Highway Department photo

A JOB HE EARNED

When Greer was promoted from district engineer at Tyler in 1936 to chief of design and construction at Austin, the Tyler newspaper ran this editorial cartoon, Nov. 13, 1936.

— Greer files

A Greer family photo in 1936. Father Sam Greer, left, holding Ann Colton Greer, sons Marcus, Dewitt and Robert Greer, and Marcus' son, standing in front of the Sam Greer home in Tyler.

-- Greer family files

Lee County Commissioner J. H. Patschke (in buggy, rear) watches early road "mainte-nance" with ox-drawn scraper, early 1900s.

— Department files

Here's how freight was carried to many Texas communities before motor vehicles and highways changed transportation. This is a train of oxen-drawn covered wagons. This scene was in Central Texas about the 1850s. Horses and mules also were used widely for transportation in developing America.

— Highway Department photo

This scene from Victoria county was common on Texas "highways" in the first third of this century. "Getting Texans out of the mud" became a major goal of government and citizens.

— Highway Department photo

*This World War I surplus equipment was being used by the
Texas Highway Department in 1932, Uvalde County.*

— Highway Department files

The first Dallas-Fort Worth turnpike in the 1920s.

— Highway Department photo

A new road is launched. Note campfire cooking and "chuck wagon" box on the truck.

— Highway Department files

When Greer received a Distinguished Alumnus Award from Texas A&M in 1965. Standing is Chancellor Gibb Gilchrist. President Earl Rudder is on Greer's left.

— Highway Department photo

A restored Model T Roadster driven by Mayor Dave Abernathy of Pittsburg touring Greer's old home town Sept. 9, 1966, during "Greer Day" festivities.

— Highway Department photo

Heavy artillery moves toward Fort Hood on U.S. 84 at Evant in March 1945. Most Texas highways were inadequate for such heavy vehicles when World War II started in 1941. The department's efforts were devoted mostly to military roads for the next four years.

— Highway Department photo

Greer about 1950.

— Greer files

The boss' office. Greer about 1955.

— Greer files

Farm-to-market road program was part of the huge construction launched after World War II. By 1960 (as shown in this photo), Texas had paved thousands of miles of rural roads in addition to building its noted major highway system.

ANOTHER 1958
TRAFFIC SAFETY PROJECT
DRIVE CAREFULLY
TEXAS HIGHWAY DEPARTMENT

Safety became a major concern of highway builders. Gov. Price Daniel, left, with Greer.

Greer ponders a problem, about 1960.

— Highway Department photo

From left, Highway Commissioners Robert L. Potts, Marshall Formby and E. H. Thornton with State Engineer Greer, about 1954. Potts taught the state's first highway engineering course at Texas A&M before World War I.

— Highway Department photo

Governor Allan Shivers stands beside a state line marker which the Highway Department installed during the 1950s.

— Highway Department photo

John Connally, Governor 1962-1969, and Greer.

— Highway Department photo

Texas Highway Department border Information Centers started giving visitors anti-litter bags in 1965. Gov. John Connally, Traveler Counselor Pam Latham and Greer.

— Highway Department photo

Greer country.

— Highway Department file

Greer promoting the United Fund in 1957.

— Highway Department photo

Greer presents a resolution in 1964 to Bessie Bergstrom, the
original employee in 1917 when the Highway Department
opened with an office behind the Texas House of Representatives chamber in the capitol. Miss Bergstrom worked for the
Department for 47 years, her sister Hazel, for 42 years. Both
live in Austin.

— Highway Department photo

The Greers were guests of honor at an Anglo-Texan Society reception in London in 1954, being greeted by Sir Alfred Bossom.

— Greer family files

Greer visited London in June 1954 for highway meetings. This photo was taken at a London airport luncheon June 23, 1954, after touring the Road Research Laboratory with British highway officials.   — Greer files

The Greers, left, with Highway Commissioner and Mrs. Fred Wemple of Midland. Wemple served in 1947-1953 while Greer headed the department.

A 1962 photo. From left, Einer Juul and his wife Ann Colton Greer Juul, Mrs. Homer Garrison and her husband, Public Safety Director Garrison, and Helen Greer.

A family portrait at "Dewitt C. Greer Day" festivities in Pitts-
burg. Left to right, Son-in-law Einer Juul, daughter Ann Col-
ton, Helen and Dewitt.

A new freeway is opened about 1965.

— Highway Department photo

Lieutenant Governor Preston E. Smith, serving as "Governor for a Day" proclaimed Aug. 4, 1967, as "Dewitt C. Greer Day" after Greer announced plans to retire.

— Highway Department photo

The Texas Transportation Institute at Texas A&M, which Greer helped create, presented him an award. Left to right, President Earl Rudder, Greer and Sen. Bill Moore of Bryan.

— Highway Department photo

Lewis E. Bracey, Uvalde banker, President Rudder, and Greer give the Aggie victory sign. — Highway Department photo

When Greer returned to the Aggie campus in 1965 to be honored as a Distinguished Alumnus, he lined up again as a trombone player with the band.

— Highway Department photo

Greer opens a new highway interchange near Bryan-College Station.

Many years after Greer became head of the Texas Highway Department, Pittsburg city officials named U.S. 271, a North-South highway, after its famous son.

— Highway Department photo

Shot of the "Greer Day" proclamation in Pittsburg in 1966.

— Highway Department photo

Greer received an award from President M. L. Shadburn of the
American Association of State Highway Officials in Atlanta.

— Highway Department photo

Governor Dolph Briscoe signed a highway funding bill in 1977. Standing, left to right, State Rep. James Nugent of Kerrville (now Railroad Commissioner), Highway Commissioners Charles E. Simons, Greer, Sen. Bill Moore of Bryan, and Chairman Reagan Houston of San Antonio.

— Greer files

Dewitt and Helen Greer represented the International Roads Federation at a meeting in Tokyo, pictured with Japanese highway officials.

— Greer files

On Jan. 2, 1968, Greer "retired" from the highway department to become the first professor of engineering practice for the University of Texas-Austin Engineering Foundation. Here the new teacher is greeted by President-elect Norman Hackerman of the University.

Assistant Engineer-Director DeBerry, Engineer-Director Dingwall, Commissioners Woodward, Kultgen and Petry.

— Highway Department photo

The Alabama-Coushatta Indians of Polk county honored Highway Commissioners Greer, Charles E. Simons (with glasses) and Reagan Houston, about 1975.

— Greer files

Facing camera, left, Weldon Hart, executive vice president, Texas Good Roads Association, with Greer, about 1970.

— Greer files

Highway builders go formal in 1958, at an Associated General Contractors' banquet in Austin. Left to right, Greer, AGC President Bill Cape of Houston, Commissioner Herbert Petry, and Contractor L. P. (Pete) Gilvin of Amarillo.

— Greer files

Engineer-Director Dingwall is honored by the Commissioners Hal Woodward of Coleman (1959-1968), Herbert Petry Jr. of Carrizo Springs, and J. H. Kultgen of Waco (1963-1969).

— Highway Department photo

DEWITT CARLOCK GREER

...IN RECOGNITION AND APPRECIATION
OF THE SAGACIOUS LEADERSHIP GIVEN
THE EMPLOYEES OF THE
TEXAS HIGHWAY DEPARTMENT...

...WHOSE PERSONAL AND PROFESSIONAL LIFE
SERVES AS AN INSPIRATION TO
PAST, PRESENT AND FUTURE MEMBERS
OF THE HIGHWAY FAMILY...

PRESENTED 26 SEPTEMBER 1967
BY EMPLOYEES OF
THE TEXAS HIGHWAY DEPARTMENT

*In September 1967, Highway Department employees presented
this plaque to their retiring chief.*

— Highway Department photo

An act of the Legislature authorized naming of the highway
headquarters building for Greer.

— Highway Department photo

A plaque honoring Greer is placed inside the highway head-quarters building in 1981. Left to right, Commissioners A. Sam Waldrop, John R. Butler Jr., Robert H. Dedman, Greer, and Engineer-Director Mark Goode.

— Highway Department photo

From left, Commissioner Petry, Greer, State Highway Engineer J. C. Dingwall and Commissioner Simons, October 1972.

— Highway Department photo

Engineer-Director DeBerry and Commission member Reagan Houston of San Antonio.

— Highway Department photo

Princess Leona Sylestine of the Alabama-Coushattas presented Gov. William P. Clements Jr. with a Texas bolo tie at the State Capitol Visitor Center in August 1980, as department travel counselors watch. Counselors wear the bolos with uniforms.

— Highway Department photo

The Indian princess also gave Engineer-Director Mark Goode an official bolo tie.   — Highway Department photo

Other Highway Officials of the Greer Era

BRADY GENTRY of Tyler,
commissioner 1939-1945.
— Highway Department photo

HARRY HINES of Wichita
Falls, Commissioner 1935-
1941.
— Highway Department photo

REUBEN WILLIAMS of
Dallas, member 1941-1947.
— Highway Department photo

FRED E. KNETSCH of
Seguin, Commissioner
1943-1949.
— Highway Department photo

A. F. MITCHELL of Corsicana,
commissioner 1949-1951.
— Highway Department photo

JOHN S. REDDITT of Lufkin,
commissioner 1945-1948.
— Highway Department photo

CHARLES F. HAWN of
Athens, commissioner
1957-1963.
— Highway Department photo

GARRETT MORRIS of Fort
Worth, member, 1968-1971.
— Highway Department photo

RAY A. BARNHART of Houston, Commission member, 1979-1981.

— Highway Department photo

A. SAM WALDROP of Abilene, Commission member 1978-1983.

— Highway Department photo

Engineer-Directors Succeeding Greer

J. C. (DING) DINGWALL
1968-1973
— Highway Department photo

B. L. DeBERRY, Engineer-
Director, 1973-1980.
— Highway Department photo

MARK G. GOODE
Engineer-Director, 1980-
— Highway Department photo

The Commission in 1984

*ROBERT H. DEDMAN of
Dallas, Commission member
1981-*

— Highway Department photo

*JOHN R. BUTLER, JR., of
Houston, Commission member, 1981-*

— Highway Department photo

*ROBERT C. LANIER, of
Houston Commission Chairman, 1983-*

— Highway Department photo

Roadside rest and picnic parks are built all over Texas. This one is on Interstate Highway 35 West, four miles south of Burleson.
— Highway Department photo

Urban freeways laced Texas cities when Greer left the department in 1981. This is Southwest Freeway in Houston, Loop 610 and U.S. 59.
— Highway Department photo

Dewitt C. Greer
. . . during the 1950s

All living Texas Highway Commission members (except Kultgen) and Engineer-Directors met January 1984 in Austin to honor Clara Bewie, who retired after fifty years with the department, mostly as Commission secretary. Clara Bewie is seated beside Greer. Standing, from left, are Woodward, Dedman, Barnhart, Waldrop, Petry, Simons, Thornton, Morris, Houston, Formby, DeBerry, Butler, Goode, Hawn, and Dingwall.

10

"A Man's Work Is a Lot Easier When He Likes It."

"A long smooth stretch of Texas highway does the same thing to Dewitt Greer that a beautiful sunset does to other persons."

So wrote Garth Jones, chief of the Associated Press Bureau in Austin, reflecting on the life and skill of the state highway engineer in 1957.

" 'A highway engineeer sort of unravels with pride when he sees something that he has done for mankind.' " Greer told the reporter.[1]

At the time, under Greer's leadership, Texas had more miles of paved highway than any other state and was building new highways faster than any other place in the world.

Jones explained that Greer got his recreation studying highway maps, knew "where every mile of pavement has been laid in Texas and where the next mile should be. Co-workers are no longer surprised that Greer can recall promptly the details of a contract let fourteen years ago, down to the exact thickness of the pavement slab."

Greer explained simply his zeal for highway-building: "A man's work is a lot easier when he likes it."

After Greer's first seventeen years as department head, he was described as "obviously proud of his record . . . proud of the faith his workers have in him. . . . He sometimes describes himself as the quarterback of a team of about sixty key workers in the twenty-five districts throughout the state."

The Greer team was coached to accent the positive.

"Our philosophy has been to take about 10 percent of the time it would normally take to gripe or alibi for not doing a job — and go ahead and find a way to do the job," said Greer.[2]

The three commissioners appointed by governors always find the office stimulating.

"I don't believe I have ever found a commissioner who didn't get a bang out of public work and hate to leave although they had to get back to private life," Greer reflected.

He served as state highway engineer with fifteen commissioners during twenty-seven years: Brady Gentry of Tyler, Robert Lee Bobbitt of San Antonio, Harry Hines of Wichita Falls, Fred E. Knetsch of Seguin, John S. Redditt of Lufkin, Fred A. Wemple of Midland, A. F. Mitchell of Corsicana, Robert J. Potts of Harlingen, E. H. Thornton, Jr., of Houston, Marshall Formby of Plainview, Herbert C. Petry, Jr., of Carrizo Springs, Charles F. Hawn of Athens, Hal Woodward of Coleman, and J. H. Kultgen of Waco, and Reuben Williams of Dallas.

After his appointment to the Highway Commission in April, 1969, by Gov. Preston Smith, Greer was a colleague of another six commission members.

They were Petry, Morris, Charles E. Simons of Austin (then of Dallas), A. Sam Waldrop of Abilene, Reagan Houston of San Antonio, and Ray A. Barnhart of Houston.

Once Publisher Charles K. Devall of Kilgore headed a delegation from his city to seek highway construction money. Devall and Greer are old friends from East Texas, and the publisher had actively supported the highway program and Greer through the Texas Good Roads Association.

When the arguments to the commission ended, Greer asked:

"Charley, all you want is what you're entitled to, isn't it?"

"No," replied Devall, "—like everybody else, we want all we can get."[3]

Devall also recalled that in later years, Greer once warned a group of small-city and rural-oriented citizens to watch out for urban domination of highway funds and construction, at the expense of less populous places. Greer's prediction seems sound, in the light of the later emphasis on expensive metropolitan freeway and mass transit. Even the major interstate highways began to suffer from heavy traffic and inadequate funds for maintenance.

Commissioners almost unanimously found Greer ideal by temperament and training for the task at hand.

One of Greer's most enthusiastic supporters is Marshall Formby.

"Dewitt and I have been working together for years," said Formby. "When I was county judge of one of the smallest counties in the state (Dickens), I would come to Austin and he would listen to my problems. When I was a state senator I would bring delegations over and he would listen to their problems.

"No matter how busy he is, Dewitt always has time to listen to highway problems."[4]

Although many local officials and delegations wanting highways constructed, designated, or put into long-range plans failed to get approval, Greer usually had a way of sending them away politely and with the feeling the man was really interested in their problems. Even the most obscure visitor was treated with respect, and Greer often suggested that some alternative might be worked out.

Formby described a commission member's role as "wonderfully satisfying" even though time-consuming and demanding.

"You see a lot of Texas and get to know what Texans are like all over the state," Formby said.[5]

Even in tight spots, Greer's sense of humor prevailed.

"My great delights were the occasional opportunities I had to travel alone with Dewitt," recalled Reagan Houston, commission chairman 1973-79 with Greer as a fellow-member. Greer's tenure on that body started April 1, 1972, and lasted until he retired March 23, 1981.

Greer particularly came alive when traveling into his beloved East Texas.

"I could detect a change in his dialect as soon as we started east,' Houston said. "By the time we reached our (East Texas) destination, he was one of them again.

"Once we were flying from Austin to a meeting at College Station. I was sitting in the co-pilot's seat and Dewitt was behind me. There were scattered thundershowers and we were on instruments. We hit the worst bump I ever had in a plane, and when I recovered I turned to see how Dewitt had fared. He was obviously shaken and had lost his hat.

"When I inquired how he was doing, his only response was 'Damn that Travis Long (then district engineer at Austin) — he's got to fix those chug holes!' "[6]

Greer practiced a policy of keeping money invested, rather than idle. Highway funds, he contended, should be invested in road improvements just as quickly as the cash became available and it was the Highway Department's job to be ready to build.

Others marveled at how fast Texans got going on the huge post-World War II expansion program.

"Our policy," explained Greer, "—when we get the money put it under the rubber. I'm a believer in being broke when the time for new money comes around."

Texans hardly needed appetites whetted for highway construction.

Greer took a lot of ribbing because the department
often erected large signs announcing that a new superhighway would be built along a certain route just as soon
as money became available. Some of them were put up
even before the Federal Highway Act authorized billions
for construction.

"Here would be a little old shirt-tail road with 300
feet right-of-way, the fences moved back and signs saying there would be a big highway some day. We took a
lot of kidding and we took a chance. But it paid off,"
Greer said.[7]

"Men at Work" signs rapidly replaced the billboards
of hope after World War II.

Greer summed it up:

"The 1950s and 1960s were the most dramatic years
in the history of highway construction in Texas. The Age
of the Freeway dawned in the 1950s. By the mid-1960s
superhighways were part of the everyday life of Texans in
every corner of the state.

"Rapid growth of Texas major cities was inseparably
linked with highway development. The first large movement toward the suburbs occurred in the years immediately after World War II, when highway facilities were
extended to serve them. Many cities and towns around
the great urban centers owed their existence to their
proximity to good highway facilities.

"The era also witnessed the decline of older modes of
transportation and a growing dependence on highways.
More than 1,800 Texas communities were served by no
system of transportation other than the highway network (by) 1965. Impetus was given to highway development throughout the nation in 1956 with the beginning
of the National System of Defense and interstate highways. Popularly called the interstate highway system,
this network is the world's greatest public works project. Scheduled for completion in the 1970s, the inter-

state system was conceived as a system of 41,000 miles, linking nearly every major population center in the nation. All routes on the network were to be constructed as controlled-access traffic arteries, with no stop lights or stop signs and no crossing at grade."[8]

Of the 41,000 miles of superhighway across the nation, Texas' designation was 3,027 miles. Before Greer ended his career with the Highway Department in 1979, after serving as commissioner and chairman, nearly all of this interstate highway system was built. Since an expressway takes twenty or more years to plan and complete, these popular arteries loaded with trucks and smaller vehicles gave future highway administrators and commissions an imposing task of maintenance, as did the thousands of miles of other roads on which millions of motorists travel billions of miles a year.

While Greer became best-known to the public as a can-do Aggie directing the construction of the world's greatest highway system, he also was a superb engineer esteemed by fellow professionals.

His major concern in building highways was safety. To Greer, each fatality was a tragedy. His mother died in a West Texas traffic accident caused by a drunk driver.

The best efforts never succeeded in stopping the carnage, but the battle to reduce the toll was unceasing.

"Department engineers constantly strive to design accident-proof highways," Greer reminded THD employees. "Failing to in this, they do the next best thing: 'design for safer accidents.' "[9]

Under Greer's administration, minimum width of two-lane pavement was increased from twenty to twenty-six feet, the widest required by any state. Texas also pioneered construction of wide shoulders along its highways, so vehicles could safely get off the road.

As truck loads increased from 7,000 pounds in the 1930s to almost unlimited loads based on axle strength, so were much stronger roadbeds needed. Roads used for military purposes during the 1940s training period proved so flimsy it was necessary to replace thousands of miles for heavier travel as time and money permitted.[10]

Most early "highway" engineers had been educated as civil engineers and trained largely to construct railroads.

The first "highway" accommodated motor vehicles built for driving thirty-five or forty miles an hour in a light car where drivers rode much higher than in low-slung later models. At such height and slow speed, drivers — if they minded their business — could drive safely on roads with frequent sharp turns, often with "blind corners."

This changed as the Motor Age advanced.

Greer pressed research to meet the need, and the Texas Highway Institute was founded at Texas A&M (where Gibb Gilchrist became president and later chancellor). Thomas M. MacDonald, the respected long-time director of the U.S. Bureau of Public Roads and friend of Texas highways, came to College Station when he retired in 1953 to help with the project.

While the institute's developments were numerous, one of the most publicized was the "breakaway" traffic sign. Engineers in other states liked the idea so well that eleven states joined Texas for further research and development.

The change, of course, allows the highway sign to snap on impact, giving occupants of a vehicle a good chance to survive the crash. Numerous breakaway signs are struck by errant vehicles, without causing death or serious injury. Such signs became standard on all of Texas' interstate highways.

Likewise, the department improved the heavy steel guard rails that keep vehicles from plunging to destruction in dangerous places. Ends of the railings are buried, so the vehicle will "climb" or glance off the railing rather than being impaled on open ends.

Roadside plantings also improve safety. A strategically planted shrub or tree can alert a driver to an approaching bridge or curb.

Roadside rest parks, which Texas pioneered, serve a major safety role by encouraging drivers to stop and relax — even nap — to break long trips. Texas has more than 1,100 such rest spots along its busiest highways.

Even "Drive Friendly" signs, suggested by Governor Preston Smith, help the cause of safety.

Highway design, especially freeways, plays a major role in accident control and changes continue as experience proves what works and what doesn't. It is almost impossible to foresee all the ways a driver can go wrong — such as entering an "Exit" and heading into oncoming traffic of an expressway.

In 1972, while serving as a commission member, Greer noted how new operational features help these high-traffic arteries.[11]

"A depressed freeway — one where the main freeway lanes are below the average grade of the surrounding ground — causes less unwanted sound to reach the neighborhood," Greer cited an example. "It also allows major neighborhood streets to cross it at approximately the same grade, facilitating traffic movement.

"But it operates better, simply because on entering the freeway, the entrance ramp is inclined downward, letting gravity supply a little extra momentum needed for acceleration on entering the main lanes.

"Similarly, leaving the freeway, the exit ramp is inclined upwards, slowing the vehicle naturally for its entry into the conventional street system."

Highway engineers, maintenance workers, police and lawmakers all strive unceasingly to reduce the terrible traffic toll, which exceeds the horrible slaughter of any war.

In terms of miles traveled, the struggle for safety is making progress. During three decades, including most of Greer's service as department head, highway deaths in Texas declined from an average of 16.6 for every million miles traveled to 5.6 deaths per million miles.[12]

The problem is that annual highway travel totaled an astonishing eighty-two billion miles over Texas highways in 1982 and has risen at five percent per year. Including city driving, vehicles travel more than 120 billion miles per year in Texas.[13]

Despite many imperfections, roads and vehicles became safer each year in terms of miles traveled — thanks to improved technology and equipment and dedicated efforts to keep making travel safer.

State Engineer Greer told an interviewer:[14]

"The highway system of 1946 was a casualty of World War II. The roads in place were deemed expendable to the war effort. Maintenance was down to a bare minimum, and new construction was limited to that which related directly to defense needs.

"Immediately after the war we were faced with rapid urbanization of the state, the move to the suburbs and many, many more vehicles. Twenty years ago, there were no expressways. Traffic engineering as a science did not exist. Signals were posted by 'guess and by golly' largely and supplemented where accident experience told engineers they should be.

"Now we can predict the usage of our facilities and design them accordingly. We are building our highways to handle greater traffic volumes of heavier, faster vehicles, and handle them more efficiently.

"Speaking of efficiency, the most economical type of highway is the expressway, simply because it handles more traffic more efficiently. The cost of an expressway per mile traveled on it is about 60 percent of the least costly farm road."

Parking facilities for the rapidly growing number of vehicles never was a responsibility of the Texas Highway Department in Greer's view.

"Our responsibilities have been defined by the Legislature and the Constitution. The State Highway Department receives the greater portion of its revenues from motor fuel taxes. Parked automobiles don't use gasoline.

We feel it is our responsibility to provide an even flow of traffic to and from the cities and suburban areas. . . . We will get them there and get them out. It is not our responsibility to provide the parking while they are there."

Greer never gave much support to proposals of mass transit until the Legislature authorized, at the urging of city lawmakers, that the Highway Department help develop mass transit.

"Our cities literally grew up in the age of the automobile and the highway," Greer commented. "Texas cities — and Texans themselves — are geared to the freedom of movement afforded by the highway and personal motor vehicle."[15]

As then-chairman of the commission, Greer did not object when the Legislature in 1975 changed the name to State Department of Highways and Public Transportation, the commission to the same longer title, and the state highway engineer to engineer-director. Merged into the department was the young Texas Mass Transit Commission.

Greer and other old-timers of the department never were keen about the new name, nor often used it. They still refer to it as "Highway Department" and "Highway Commission."

Despite his advocacy of expressways, Greer never lost interest in small towns and rural roads, so familiar in his early life.

The farm-to-market paving program continued from 1949 to the present, and totaled more than 40,000 miles when Greer left the commission in 1981. Paved F-M mileage totaled 41,774 on March 1, 1983.[16]

Some small-town business operators complained when highways started bypassing downtown areas, allowing through traffic to avoid the main business districts. Greer responded that the travelers passing through provided relatively little of the downtown business and much congestion. He declared downtown should be a place to transact business, and noted that new businesses to serve travelers immediately grew alongside the bypass routes.

While materials, equipment and finances improved, Greer primarily credited interested, dedicated people for developing good highways.

He fought for better pay for department employees, particularly engineers, who often worked for considerably less than those of like qualifications and experience in the federal government and private industry.

"The morale . . . the spirit of the corps . . . of the organization," he credited with being the major factor in the department's success.

"It's the greatest field of public service that an individual can enjoy today . . . service to his fellow man, which after all is what we are put here for," Greer commented at the height of his career.[17]

"At the end of each day in highway work you can see the results of your day's work, whether you are building a bridge, laying concrete pavement, maintaining a road, putting up signs. . . . You actually see and evaluate your accomplishments at the end of each and every day. . . . Our people have been free of political intrusion. Our people are employed and advanced based on merit. We put responsibility and authority together in the subordinate officers of the department all the way down into the ranks — not just responsibility, but responsibility and authority — those things go together to make a good organization.

"We do not demand that everybody do the same thing in the same way, as long as he's able to do it economically and in a satisfactory manner. We do not dictate from headquarters each and every detail.

"I think this principle brings out the very best in people. All this has built departmental morale to make our people proud to work for the Texas Highway Department and kept them working for us through the years."

Many factors work together to create a successful highway system.

Greer listed:[18]

"First, we have enjoyed the support and the confidence of the people of Texas. They have expressed this support by electing capable representatives. In this way, the highway program has had the benefit of sound legislation and financing, which is the lifeblood of any highway program.

"The people and their representatives have recognized and fought the dangers of dispersion and diversion of funds available to the highway program."

The battle to keep "road user" taxes going to highway construction, maintenance, and policing — rather than being diverted to non-highway purposes — has been continuous in Texas. Greer rose to the challenge whenever the occasion arose.

Continuing:

"This broad-based public support has made certain that the Highway Commission and Highway Department do not play politics with the people's money."

He credited the Texas Good Roads Association, composed of business and civic leaders, with keeping the state's attention focused on a goal of "Total road service — for all Texas."

One of the best public relations operatives ever on the state capital scene, Greer praised the state's media for "enormous contributions" to the highway program's success.

"They have kept Texans well-informed of the progress and problems of the program, keeping in mind the reporter's duty always is to comfort the afflicted — and to afflict the comfortable,'" Greer commented.

A great judge of people, Greer took care to know in advance something about the integrity and reliability of those with whom he discussed highways for public information. This included reporters, legislators, and others. With some he spoke with caution, but with those he knew well and trusted, Greer was completely candid.

Greer understood well the world of politics, and the importance of building grassroots support, even the subtle massaging of egos of public officials.

"Dewitt planned everything he did," remarked Garrett Morris, former commissioner.[19]

"He was very successful with the Legislature. He made it a point to encourage all chambers of commerce and highway groups to involve their representatives and senators in their requests for roads or improvements.

"Then, when the group appeared, he would personally recognize the senators and representatives and praise them before their home folks. This treatment, coupled with the fact that every community wants more roads, always kept the department and Dewitt in good standing with the Legislature."

[1] *Austin American-Statesman*, Sept. 8, 1957.
[2] Ibid.
[3] Letter to the author, July 28, 1983.
[4] Letter to the author.
[5] Ibid.
[6] Letter to the author, Apr. 20, 1983.
[7] Garth Jones article.
[8] *Handbook of Texas Supplement*, Vol. 3, p. 390, 1972.
[9] Department memo, about 1965.
[10] Golden Anniversary history, based on recollections of T. S. Huff, chief design engineer, 1967.
[11] Written for *Analogy* magazine, 1972, department files.
[12] Department files, 1966.
[13] Department files, 1966.
[14] Ibid., 1982 figures.
[15] Department files.
[16] Department files.
[17] The *Dallas Morning News*, Sept. 15, 1963.
[18] Department files, 1966.
[19] Letter to the author, Feb. 1, 1983.

11

Days of Glory

As Greer and the Texas Highway Department attracted national and international attention, so did the demands for his services.

President-elect John F. Kennedy considered Greer for the position of federal highway administrator, reportedly at the urging of Vice President-elect Lyndon B. Johnson, in December 1960. The $22,500-a-year office went to another Democrat from Missouri, replacing a Republican who had served under President Dwight D. Eisenhower.

Greer never acknowledged great interest in the federal office, except to say once it is the only position in the world he considered more important than state highway engineer in Texas.

In 1961, the Legislature and Highway Commission boosted Greer's salary a hefty $125 per year to $18,625.

News that Texas might lose his services to Washington caused some dismay in the ranks of highway supporters, who breathed relief the appointment never came.

The occasion did bring forth public tributes to Greer and the department he helped achieve a pinnacle.

"The federals couldn't have done better than if they had picked Greer," the *Brady Standard* proclaimed editorially.[1]

"In the newspaper business, we come in contact with many government agencies, and the Texas Highway Department must be one of the finest.

"They get good men, do a good job, and never has there been a hint of fraud or scandal.

"Texas Highway Department officials are courteous and polite, but no man is so big or wealthy or powerful that he could sway them to act against the taxpayers' interest. They build highways like they know they should be built — and Texans can see the result, miles and miles of well-built, well-maintained highways stretching from horizon to horizon.

"Maybe it's odd to praise an organization for being honest, but where an agency is responsible for spending millions of dollars it isn't always the easiest thing to do.

"The Highway Department is held in high regard among newspapermen throughout the state as being highly efficient, independent, and incorruptible, even while working under terrific pressure. And newspapermen watch for things like that. . . .

"The excellence of the Texas Highway Department may not be the sole responsibility of D. C. Greer, but if it were any less efficient he would get the blame. So he can take part of the credit too. Greer and his crew have done a good job for Texas."

As president, Lyndon Johnson twice made overtures to Greer to accept a top federal office — once as highway administrator and again as head of the General Services Administration. Greer declined both, but the president did appoint Frank Turner, another Texas Aggie working for the federal highway agency (whom Greer recommended), to take the administrator's post.

Both President and Mrs. Johnson had high regard for Greer and the Texas Highway Department. Within days after Johnson became president in 1963 following the assassination of John F. Kennedy, the Highway Commission designated "Ranch Road 1," along the Pedernales River from Hye to Stonewall, to serve the "Texas White House," where the Johnsons resided while in Texas.

Traffic became heavy through that area, and continued after Johnson retired, as many motorists visited the park across from the Johnson place and drove for a closer view along "Ranch Road 1."

Mrs. Johnson became very active in promoting roadside beauty along Texas highways, and annually gave awards to the responsible people in districts which excelled in beautification.

The activity was coordinated through the Highway Department, which had pioneered highway roadside planting during the 1930s.

Demands on Greer's time and energy increased as the department's accomplishments under his guidance became known outside Texas.

He was elected president of the Western Association of State Highway Officials in 1953, and later as president of the American Association of State Highway Officials. The latter organization presented him its two most prestigious awards — the George S. Bartlett Award in 1953 and the Thomas MacDonald Award in 1964. In 1962, Greer was among ten "Top Public Works Men of the Year" selected by Kiwanis International and the American Public Works Association.

Greer served three times as official U.S. delegate to International Roads Federation conferences. He traveled widely, both at home and abroad, nearly always on business.

Wife Helen accompanied Greer on many of these trips. A dainty, gracious lady, she had many friends and was active in church and social work in Austin. Their daughter, Ann Colton, married Einer Juul, an Austin banker, and the couple has two sons, Dewitt and Craig.

While Greer was devoted to his family, his main life was connected with highways. The Greers attended the

First Methodist Church in downtown Austin and sat in the same pew every Sunday. Greer served as treasurer of the church and is credited with being "as careful with the church's money as with his own."

Greer never displayed much interest in yard work, but the family often sat together in the yard in the evening.

While living on Jarratt Avenue in West Austin, before moving to the Mount Barker address, the Greers owned a fox terrier dog named Fritz, the same name as the dog who hunted with the Greer brothers back in Pittsburg years before.

A neighbor on Jarratt, Gibson Randle, said the Greer dog was the best-behaved animal in the area.

"When Dewitt took the dog outside, and told it not to cross the sidewalk, his dog never crossed the sidewalk, but stayed right on the lawn," Randle reported.

Asked later how he disciplined his dog so well, Greer replied:

"I trained him to stay in the yard by beating his butt."

Occasionally, Greer spent an evening at poker with Austin friends from outside the Highway Department. He is described as an excellent, careful poker-player who never got into high-stakes games.

Greer enjoyed hunting trips, but seldom shot anything. He liked camp life as relaxation from Highway Department duties and in later years went annually to Dolph Briscoe's Catarina Ranch with a few old friends.

Deer hunting had little appeal for Greer, who did occasionally hunt quail. His accident of being wounded in the rear by a shotgun pellet didn't discourage Greer from enjoying such trips, but he was never enthusiastic about the exercise of hunting.

Reading was Greer's lifelong recreation. He read newspapers regularly and kept up with literature affecting his work.

Devoted to the Methodist Church from childhood,

Greer served in church positions even during his busiest
years. He was on the pulpit committee which brought
Dr. Marvin Vance, a well-known conservative preacher,
to the First Methodist Church in Austin as pastor; and
Greer served on the building committee.

Likewise, Greer was active in the Rotary Club and
presented programs usually related to highways. The
Shriners organization was another interest.

He spoke at many professional gatherings across
the United States and abroad, ranging from Norway to
Australia, invited by those who had heard the fame of
the Texas highway program.

In 1958, Yale University appointed him to the advisory committee of its Bureau of Highway Traffic, promoting teaching and research into highway matters.

Although he became an international figure in the
highway world, Greer never strayed far from his roots.

He was twice honored by his hometown of Pittsburg, an always joyous occasion for him.

Once Greer declared his early days in East Texas
were the happiest of his life. Of his career, Greer said:[2]

"Being employed by the Texas Highway Department
has been a great experience. . . . I suppose I enjoyed my
work as district engineer of District 10 at Tyler the most.
As a district engineer, I enjoyed working with people. You
see, I love people and enjoyed hiring young engineers or
any other employee and watching them grow."

Pittsburg, Tyler, and College Station always held
special places in Greer's memory book. In 1966, Pittsburg celebrated "Dewitt C. Greer Day." A reception was
held at the country club. Mayor D. H. Abernathy presented a laudatory proclamation:[3] "Due and considered
notice has been taken of the worldwide recognition of an
almost-native son of Pittsburg and Camp County — Dewitt Carlock Greer.

"Who is recognized as the highway engineer without peers in all the world, the universe and outer space."

Its famous near-native was designated as Ambassador Extraordinary by the mayor who charged Greer with "the weighty responsibility of spreading the fame of Pittsburg and Camp County far and wide, as he travels the globe."[4]

Greer did little special promotion of his boyhood home. When U.S. Highway 271 was constructed inside Pittsburg, and named "Dewitt C. Greer Boulevard," the honored one insisted the road was improved because it deserved to be done, not because he was state highway engineer. Nevertheless, he was pleased at the designation.

The home folks insisted Greer was on their side. County Judge Earl Julian commented Greer "has done a good job in our area and especially on Texas 11 (crossing the county east to west and connecting with oil-field areas in both directions). I feel he is responsible for us getting that highway."

On completing thirty-five years with the department on July 31, 1962, Greer was surprised at a ceremony honoring him arranged by the commission.[5]

Department employees, contractors, legislators, delegations scheduled for hearing by the commission that day, and others filled the big hearing room. Guests included John Connally, the Democratic nominee for governor, formerly secretary of the navy under President Kennedy. In November, Connally was elected to his first of three two-year terms.

Chairman Petry noted the event was supposed to be kept from Greer's knowledge until the day of the ceremony but "Dewitt knows what's going on all over Texas and the nation, for that matter, and it's impossible to keep anything secret from him."

Assistant State Highway Engineer Dingwall told the audience that Greer's ability was unquestionably great, but his greatest quality was "loyalty."

"Throughout the year," he said, "disciplinary cases come up with employees, all sorts of matters of a man making a mistake, some error — as much work as we do, many errors creep in. I have always known Mr. Greer to lean over backwards to take the position of the employee when it comes to working out some relationship with the employees of the department."

"Outstanding leadership" by Greer was praised by commission member Hal Woodward. He said this applied both to leadership of the department's 16,000 employees and the guidance Greer gave to the commission.

"We are so far ahead of other state highway departments, there is no comparison," added Commissioner Charles Hawn. "That sounds like a Texas brag, but it's on the record (he cited rapid construction of the new interstate system in Texas).

"At the same time our average cost is 'way, 'way down . . . we get more for our tax dollar in our highway system than in most any other system or department we have."

Chairman Petry summarized:

"He has so conducted his life, his personal life, his professional life, his public life — as to truly merit the trust and confidence the people of this state and the leaders in the highway field in this nation and all over the world have placed in him . . . an outstanding administrator, a man of unimpeachable integrity, the best example of a public servant. . . ."

Petry said the recognition extended throughout the nation and internationally, and was without partisanship.

"We on the commission, all being University of Texas graduates, have learned that you can work with a Texas A&M graduate — if you must!" quipped Petry. "He has certainly been loyal to Texas A&M."

Greer wisecracked that he wished the commission would stick with the agenda that he had prepared for the day — a schedule of hearings of delegations seeking highways.

He called the previous remarks "quite extravagant."
"I came from small-town people. My people were from Pittsburg, Texas; my mother's people were from Winnsboro . . . They are rather small towns, were then and still are.

"There was something though that came into that heritage, that must have been inherited by me — of a desire to serve my fellow man. Now that seems to be fundamental to all of us, but it's particularly true when you come from sort of country communities.

"I am full of gratitude, particularly today. Texas shouldn't thank me — I should thank Texas. I should thank the State; I should thank the people of this state, the highway commissioners, the legislatures, and others, who have given me the privilege of serving my fellow man for these thirty-five years."

Greer still had five years to serve as state highway engineer, and his fame continued to increase.

One prized recognition was "Man of the Year" among Texas A&M alumni in 1964. By that date, the Texas Highway Department's 65,000-mile network was recognized worldwide as the finest in existence.

Greer had supervised the spending of $4.5 billion of the taxpayer's money without a hint of scandal in the operation.

The "secret" — really an obvious fact — of Greer's success he explained in 1963 to the American Association of State Highway Officials, which Greer once served as president and for many years was an active participant.

His subject was "Truth — An Ally in a Tight Situation."[6]

"The ideal would be not to get into hot water in the first place," Greer advised.

"(This) is not altogether realistic. We (nationally) are building 41,000 miles of interstate highways that are revolutionizing our way of life. We are building them throughout the reaches of our land. We are dealing with astronomical sums of money and all the diversities and

perversities of human nature as we build. Ours is the
most extensive, the most expensive, construction enter-
prise ever undertaken by man. To accomplish this mission without the sting of criticism would be to confound
probability. . . ."

Using a term his audience understood well, Greer
recommended "preventive maintenance" to avoid trouble, cultivating good public relations.

A good image, based on reputations built on small
deeds done well over a long period, he called the ultimate
response to unwarranted criticism. "Bending the truth
can do untold damage."

An organization's image, he continued, reflects individual acts at every level.

"A company is judged by the people it keeps," Greer
reversed a common saying. "Good public relations is the
aggregate impression created by the actions and atti-
tudes of *people* on behalf of the corporate body."

A public employee, Greer quoted Thomas Jefferson,
"should consider himself public property."

"It never hurts to remind ourselves that we who build
highways work under a public mandate. If we do not have
the public's confidence, we cannot do our work."

"Truth," explained Greer "is seldom absolute. Pilate
knew this when he asked the classic question 'What is
truth?' Any good newsman knows this too. I have found
that news people, whose mission is a quest for the truth,
almost always will tell all sides of a story when the facts
are presented to them clearly and honestly."

Greer expressed doubt that it is always necessary,
or even wise, to respond to baseless or unreasonable criticism.

"We denigrate ourselves and our departments when
we — who move mountains — push the panic button at
the confrontation of a mole-hill.

"Over the years, a highway department which has
proved consistently trustworthy achieves a stature that
is virtually unassailable . . . (but) you simply can't please
everybody."

Public confidence and support, he said, "like a highway must be built from the bottom up. . . . As every Marine is a public relations man for the Corps, we would like for every employee of the Texas Highway Department to serve a good-will function . . . A friendly 'Howdy' from a flag man to a passing motorist multiplied 15,000 times may create a lot of good will.

"Our philosophy is that good engineering is not enough. Public support is essential too. The public must be informed on highway progress and highway needs. An informed public is a supporting public. 'Esprit de corps' is very important, too.

"It's axiomatic that a Texan will brag about anything. But Texans, and we think they are enlightened on the subject, are very proud of their highways, and they don't hesitate to tell others. One reason they're proud, we think, is that our Highway Department employees are proud of their jobs. They express this pride in the attitude they convey to others. . . .

"Regular service is always better than a major overhaul (cheaper too, in the long run!). Public relations, like a lubricant, can best be used to *keep* out of trouble, rather than *get* out of trouble."

Greer said public support for highways must be cultivated from the grassroots and are aided by local groups such as chambers of commerce and good roads organizations.

"Human nature wants to belong, to be part of. It wants to participate in good causes — and we emphasize that a highway program is a good cause. We are humble enough to admit that any success of our organization is a compliment to the supporters, the people of our state. We give credit generously for their assistance.

Credit also needs to be shared with the private contracting industry, which Greer regularly included as essential to the successful Texas highway program.

Keeping your word is also critical, said Greer.

"We never show favoritism, nor do for one what we wouldn't do for another. We have always considered our word, our bond, and once an agreement is reached we will carry out our portion regardless."

Coping with a crisis becomes almost impossible, unless the individual or organization bears a good reputation.

Greer suggested frequent checkups in the public relations area to foresee any problems developing.

"Let us remember that good will, like a good name, is built by many good deeds—but it may be lost by a bad one.

"It is our works, not our words, by which we are judged ultimately."

[1] Jan. 13, 1961.
[2] Department files quoting the Pittsburg newspaper, about 1975.
[3] Ibid.
[4] Ibid.
[5] Transcript from department files, July 31, 1962.
[6] Delivered Oct. 23, 1963, at Portland, Oregon; text from department files.

12

The Master Steps Aside

"AUSTIN. The Texas Highway Commission announced today that D. C. Greer, State Highway Engineer, has submitted his resignation effective July 31 in anticipation of retirement."

The news release in late July 1967 shook the state capital although nearly everybody knew of Greer's long service and that state law required retirement at age sixty-five.

Nevertheless, the state government and Texans had come to consider Greer such a fixture, and so good at his job, they hoped he could go on forever.

Chairman Petry announced that the commission — including members Woodward and Kultgen — had persuaded Greer to continue until December 31 to ease the transition to J. C. Dingwall as the new state highway engineer. Nine of Dingwall's thirty-nine years with the department had been as Greer's assistant and the two had worked closely together.

Greer's sixty-fifth birthday fell on July 27.

The year 1967 also marked the fiftieth anniversary of the Highway Department's founding, and Dewitt Greer was clearly the person most identified with its history and high reputation. Celebrations around Texas marked the year.

The Legislature in March 1967 took note of Greer's age and adopted a resolution by Sen. Charles F. Herring of Austin authorizing the commission to extend Greer's service as head of the department past the regular date. Greer chose to resign.

Yet his career was far from finished. After completing the year as state highway engineer, Greer later became a distinguished professor at the University of Texas, and concluded with twelve years as member of the Texas Highway Commission.

In announcing Greer's impending departure as administrator, Chairman Petry observed: [1]

"Mr. Greer's long association with highway matters — particularly at the national level — makes it imperative that we have the benefit of his experience in the critical months ahead.

"This is a period of great change. The role of highways in the new national Department of Transportation has not been clearly defined. Highway programs to follow completion of the interstate highway system are being formulated. Legislation affecting every highway department and every highway program throughout the nation is being prepared for presentation to Congress.

"For many years Mr. Greer has taken a leading role in development of legislative matters for the American Association of State Highway Officials, and organization which he has served as president and which he now serves as member of its executive committee."

The commission expressed regret at the fact that age made the loss of Greer's services inevitable.

The commission also voiced complete confidence in Dingwall's ability to administer the department according to the standards of excellence and the policies molded under Greer and Gibb Gilchrist.

"Through the years Mr. Greer has developed a strong

and effective organization. Loyal and capable leaders in responsible positions throughout the department will carry on and assist Mr. Dingwall in an orderly transition of responsibility and authority."

The announcement noted Dingwall was instrumental in developing the freeway systems of Texas, which were becoming a highest priority in construction. He became assistant state highway engineer in 1958, after heading the Fort Worth-Dallas Turnpike project and the department's road design division.

Despite Greer's close ties and friendship with his successor, who admired Greer greatly, the occasion must have been a wrench for one whose life had been so totally dedicated to the service of the Texas Highway Department and its citizens.

Many Texans had come to identify it as "Greer's department" as well as "The best highway department in the world."

The year 1967 was a year of celebration tinged with regret that Greer's impending retirement meant the end of an era for the Texas Highway Department. The system now totaled nearly 68,000 miles of paved highway, and Greer's administration alone had seen four and one-half billion dollars of the taxpayers' money invested in this greatest construction accomplishment in history.

Earlier at a ceremony honoring Greer at "the College" — Texas A&M — Executive Vice President Weldon Hart of the Texas Good Roads Association had saluted Greer on behalf of the public:

"Greer never lost sight of his primary purpose: giving the highway user a good honest road for his tax pennies and dollars. . . . Everywhere, in all ways, he has been outstanding for his talent, tact, wit, and unconditional integrity. I think of him in the terms used by the poet Robert Louis Stevenson in describing another person as 'steel-true and blade-straight.' And I add my own observation: with just the right touch of velvet."[2]

On September 26, 1967, Greer was the star of a "Fiftieth Anniversary Celebration" for the Highway Department at the Municipal Auditorium in Austin.

Former Governor Shivers, then president of the United States Chamber of Commerce, Francis C. Turner, director of the United States Bureau of Public Roads, and Gov. John Connally spoke glowingly of the Highway Department and Dewitt Greer. Shivers and Pete Gilvin of Amarillo, a leader among Texas highway contractors presented a $50,000 check to President Earl Rudder to finance engineering scholarships at Texas A&M.

Greer would never accept any gift of value from highway contractors or materials suppliers, and their donations in appreciation of the man went instead into scholarships.

Soon after the scholarships were established at Texas A&M, and Greer had become a professor of engineering practice at the University of Texas at Austin, friends endowed a professorship in his honor at the latter institution.

As Greer's retirement as highway administrator approached, this writer added a personal note to his old friend and frequent news source:[3]

"Although we knew it was coming, the announcement of Dewitt Greer's impending retirement brings genuine regret to all citizens who are interested in good government.

"To a very large extent, this state's magnificent system of highways stands as a monument to the dedication, ability, and integrity of this man.

"In the words of show business, Dewitt Greer will be a hard act to follow, although his successor, J. C. Dingwall is an engineer and administrator of proven great capacity.

"Greer never accepted personal credit for the success of the Texas Highway Department.

" 'These are the men who made it great,' Greer said of the department's 16,000 employees. 'In my opinion, ours is the finest single organization under any flag. Its esprit de corps is the highest in the nation.' "

"Greer spoke the truth too. While many Americans look down on public service, Greer and others like him make it respected and respectable. In many states, highway construction and maintenance has been scandalous. But it has not been in Texas since the early days of the department.

"This may be a tribute to the Legislature's wisdom in creating an agency which has considerable autonomy and is relatively removed from politics. The three highway commissioners are appointed by the governor, but the actual administration of the million-dollar-per-day spending program has been supervised by Dewitt Greer.

"A diplomat who likes dealing with politicians as well as with the public, Greer has successfully defended his department against political interference, while Texas enjoys the lowest motor fuel tax in the nation as well as the most and best highways. . . ."

Recalling his early experiences, including the rough spots and difficulties, Greer concluded:

"I wouldn't take a million dollars for them."

The recognition of Greer's career reflected credit on all public employees who had given honest and effective service, while the misdeeds of others — before and since — receive most of the public's attention.

During the Watergate scandals of 1973 during President Nixon's administration, a prominent Austin minister, the Rev. Charles A. Sumners, preached on the subject. His sermon was inserted in the *Congressional Record* by Congressman J. J. (Jake) Pickle of Austin.[4]

The minister of the historic St. David's Episcopal Church, one of the oldest in Texas, spoke of the ouster of Vice President Spiro Agnew as the Washington scandal unfolded:

". . . Part of the tragedy is that the events in the life of this prominent politician reflect upon all men in public life. This is unfair, but a truth. Many men and women in

public office have often withstood the pressures put
upon them. . . .

"One in particular comes to mind — Dewitt Greer (by
then chairman of the Texas Highway Commission). . . .
At no time has there ever been any indication of any sort
of graft or taking of bribes. A man of honor and ability,
Dewitt Greer is a distinguished public servant. . . ."

The minister contended our system of government
needs a better way to insulate its officials from the temp-
tations to use public office for private gain. This observer
feels that is visionary, although a commendable objective.

Character, such as exemplified by Dewitt Greer,
comes from inner strength and training in the difference
between right and wrong, beginning in childhood. It is
not acquired by statute, nor can the public be adequately
protected by paying government officials and employees
handsomely or by passing laws against greedy behavior.
Good salaries are vital, but only part of the package
needed to guarantee good performance by public employees.

Writers and speakers rose to superlatives as Greer
prepared to leave his long-held position.

"There's nothing left for him but canonization," an
associate was quoted.[5]

The same article commented:

"The man most responsible for the matchless Texas
highway system combines the certainty of a mathemati-
cian, the quiet air of a college professor, and the leadership of a Robert E. Lee."

While praise and honors were being heaped upon
him, Greer still ate lunch at an Austin cafeteria, occupied the same pew each Sunday with his family at the
First Methodist Church, and sat in the yard at home
with Helen and the Juuls when he had the opportunity.

Texas newspapers expressed appreciation that
Greer was staying at the helm until the end of 1967.

"It is quite easy to understand the highway commissioners' wish to keep Greer around for five months be-

yond his retirement age," the *Lubbock Avalanche-Journal* editorialized.

". . . As the commissioners pointed out, there are critical months ahead in federal-state highway relations, in connection with which his prestige and knowledge will be invaluable.[6]

"It is also good that his designated successor and chief assistant, J. C. Dingwall, is credited with all the necessary qualifications for the job. One of them is his supervision of the 'model' freeway system, experience which will be applied. . . ."

Although one associate declared, "God is a hard act to follow," Greer's legacy continued under the veterans who had worked with him in building the department.

An alumnus of Southern Methodist University, and like Greer a man of wit as well as wisdom, Dingwall drew high marks as an administrator and engineer.

Contractor Pete Gilvin of Amarillo declared:[7]

"The greatest engineering ever done was Dingwall's on the Dallas-Fort Worth toll road. He got the contract, bought the right-of-way, and built the road in less than three years. Today, it takes at least seven years to get any federal aid job done."

Dingwall took leave from the department to direct the toll road project for Texas Turnpike Authority, a new agency financed by revenue bonds to be repaid from fees paid by motorists. After the toll road opened in 1957, Dingwall returned to the department. He served as state highway engineer from 1968 until retirement in 1973.

If there ever was any jealousy among Greer's successors over being compared to their famous predecessor, it never showed. Each put a personal imprint on the department and the highway system, but the policies which guided Greer remained largely intact.

As his right-hand man, Dingwall had more opportunity to observe the special touches Greer put into running the department, such as reshuffling the minutes (proposed orders) when he offered one which met opposition within the commission.

Dingwall's successor, B. L. (Luther) DeBerry noted that "nobody ever got close to Mr. Greer" in the department, even though the DeBerrys were the Greers' next-door neighbors during the later years of Greer's career.

DeBerry headed the Highway Department from February 1973 until July 1980 while Greer served on the commission.

"He made the transition from engineer to the commission as easily as it could have been done," DeBerry commented. "When he took over as chairman of the commission, he didn't interfere with the department at all. His role was strictly policy. Some other commission members had trouble staying out of the department's business.

"Mr. Greer said he would never interfere, and that if he ever got onto my side (administration), to tell him. He never interfered." [8]

In his forty-four years with the department, DeBerry had many dealings with Greer, all strictly business until the years when as neighbors they sometimes attended professional meetings and socials together.

Like Dingwall, DeBerry worked years in the field, including building urban freeways. He spent eight years as district engineer in Dallas.

"We built a lot of freeways there and built them fast," DeBerry recalled. Now you've got to have a lot of hearings. These don't really change things but it takes a lot longer."

In times of inflation, such as the era of 1960s and 1970s, such prolonged negotiations cost taxpayers dearly as prices of right-of-way and construction escalated.

DeBerry's successor was Mark G. Goode, another product of the Greer administration.

"Mr. Greer set the pace for our department," said Goode. "His ideas and basic philosophy, his integrity, fairness, and his deep desire to maintain high quality construction standards have become a major influence on this department. These concerns and mandates have been incorporated into our basic policy over the years and remain the standards by which we serve.[9]

"His emphasis on quality construction standards cannot be overemphasized. He insisted on using Texas tax dollars on basic construction with a minimum of 'frills' and unnecessary details."

Goode said the department still follows the Greer gospel:

"Put the money in the roadway."

Another policy which Greer's successors kept intact is communication and cooperation with cities and counties in solving motor traffic problems.

Greer's successors even continued his policy of using the fewest words possible.

"One of Mr. Greer's strongest attributes was his ability to express himsellf in few words and through leadership by example. He was a firm believer in the delegation of authority to individuals and then allowing them to carry out his orders and suggestions using their own judgment," Goode continued.

"The Highway Department was Mr. Greer's career and vocation . . . But the department was also one of the great loves of his life.

"He eschewed normal hobbies such as hunting and fishing, and instead put enormous energies into making our department one of the world leaders in transportation planning and design. He wanted to carry out the best transportation system possible.

"He was indeed the premier highway engineer of his age. Today's department is firmly rooted in the basic philosophy of D. C. Greer. And we intend to carry out and maintain these basic concepts."

One of Greer's admirers is former Governor Price Daniel, who considered the highway builder without peer as a public administrator.

Reflecting on the qualities which marked this man, Daniel commented:[10]

". . . Among talents which marked his success was the tact and diplomacy with which he mixed his facts. He was always a gentleman. Even when he presented facts which did not please his listeners, he did it in a way that was not offensive. He always knew his lessons well. In many conferences I had with him, I have never seen him unprepared. In public hearings, it was the same way. . . .

"With this same ability, he caused those who worked under him to respect and admire his work and his decisions. He had the ability to say no in the most pleasant manner possible. I never saw him leave a meeting or hearing without convincing those present that he had studied or would study the highway problem and be helpful if possible."

Daniel noted that Greer was more tactful than his predecessor, Gibb Gilchrist. Daniel dealt with both men as a legislator from Liberty County, and later with Greer as speaker of the house, attorney general, and governor.

Whereas Gilchrist might leave highway delegations with bruised feelings over his manner of rejection, Greer sent them away in a more pleasant mood. Daniel appeared before both men with delegations seeking highway construction, and he credited diplomacy as being the major difference between two able administrators.

[1] Department files.

[2] *Texas Highways* magazine, February 1967, p. 16.

[3] *Dallas News*, Aug. 1, 1967.

[4] *Congressional Record*, Nov. 7, 1973.

[5] *Amarillo News*, Aug. 17, 1967, by Associated Press, Robert Heard.

[6] Aug. 3, 1967.

[7] Interview, 1983.

[8] Interview, 1983.

[9] Letter to the author, July 29, 1983.

[10] Letter to the author, Aug. 16, 1983.

13

Professor Greer

"The Department of Civil Engineering and the Center for Highway Research of the University of Texas at Austin are pleased to announce the addition of Mr. D. C. Greer to their staff, as Professor of Engineering Practice, following his retirement from the Texas Highway Department Jan. 1, 1968."[1]

This announcement two months before Greer retired from his position as state highway engineer brought some smiles, just as Gibb Gilchrist's departure thirty years earlier to become dean of engineering at Texas A&M.

After all, Gilchrist was a university "tea-sip" joining his alma mater's arch-rival.

For Greer, it was the reverse. No redder-blooded Texas Aggie ever lived than Dewitt Greer, and he was moving his expertise onto the campus of the state university.

Characteristically, Greer dismissed the matter with a quip:

"After all, we Aggies must share with our less fortunate brethren. Besides, UT is only four minutes from my home in Austin. A&M is a bit further."[2]

Among those most pleased by the appointment were Charles and Lyde Devall of Kilgore, old friends from Kilgore, who had suggested to UT Chancellor Harry Ransom that Greer be offered a distinguished professor position just as soon as he became available.[3]

Numerous university people had a similar idea about the same time.

Dr. Norman Hackerman, the university's president-elect, welcomed Greer to the faculty as the first recipient of a professorship in engineering practice, provided by the University Engineering Foundation.

During the university's centennial celebration of the 1980s, a permanent Dewitt C. Greer Professorship in Transportation Engineering was established at the school, financed by $100,000 raised by L. P. (Pete) Gilvin of Amarillo and Richard McKinney of Nacogdoches, contractors and university alumni, and other long-time friends of Greer.

The new professor offered an extra dimension to the engineering program, both from his fame as a highway builder and an administrator.

Some friends started calling him "Dr. Greer." Greer held an honorary doctorate from Texas Christian University, but ended his academic career with the engineering degree at Texas A&M. He served on an advisory board at Yale University.

"Professor Greer is bringing the world of practice into the classroom," explained Dr. Clyde Lee, director of the Center for Highway Research.[4]

"I know of no other class like it in the United States, and certainly I know of no one who is better qualified in his field."

Greer avoided the textbook approach.

He directed the course on highway administration and finance to cover current problems faced by men and women in the highway departments. There was no shortage of classroom subjects.

"The first two semesters I was thinking 'highways' but gradually my concepts about transportation began to change," said Greer.[5]

"As I pondered the urban transportation problem, I asked myself, 'is there another answer other than taking people out of their cars and putting them on buses and trains?' I decided to add the question to my list for term papers."

His was a discussion course which did not necessarily seek to come up with final solutions — rather an exchange of ideas among students and a man who had spent forty-five years building roads and operating a large program.

There were no final examinations. Greer tried to get the students to talk at least half of the class time. Students were graded according to class participation and on term papers which Greer described as "challenges."

Included were such subjects as:

"Should the state and federal governments enter the field of parking motor vehicles?"

(With the Texas Highway Department, Greer contended parking was a local problem. It was the state's responsibility to get vehicles into and between towns safely and efficiently.)

"What are the advantages and disadvantages of changing a state highway department into a state department of transportation?"

(Although this was done later by the Texas Legislature, Greer disliked the idea. Like parking, he considered mass transit in urban areas to be a local problem.)

"Will the internal combustion engine in motor vehicles be replaced in the near future?"

(Despite petroleum shortages during the 1970s which developed much research in other fuels, the internal combustion engineer with improved efficiency remained the world standard.)

"What is the proper or ideal relationship between a city government and a state highway department?"

(Cities increasingly seek state and federal funds to finance local projects.)

"How can a highway department attract engineering graduates and hold them?"

(As department heads, Greer and his successors turned to much better salaries and retirement programs than prevailed earlier, plus job stability.)

Greer also taught how the department which he helped to build administered so well through much local autonomy and responsibility to district engineers, and the division of authority within the headquarters staff.

The question of interstate and international financing and construction of highways was discussed. The United States already had taken a lead in developing the Pan-American Highway which crossed Texas en route to Mexico City and points south. In World War II, an heroic engineering feat was accomplished by the rapid construction of a military road through Western Canada to Alaska, the so-called Alcan Highway.

Greer's class sat around a large table and engaged in seminar-type discussions. He had recommended the group of students, nearly all graduates, be limited to ten, but at times a few more were accepted.

In 1971, his fall class included a senior highway design engineer from the Texas Highway Department, an engineer from the Federal Highway Administration, Austin's city traffic engineer, a planner from the Governor's Office; three air force officers, two foreign students, a former employee of the Utah Highway Department, two research engineers, and a former contractor.

". . . It was with a sense of sharing," Greer's approach was described.[6]

Greer liked teaching. It offered a sounding board from which he also learned "the younger viewpoint . . . a cross-check of young, sharp brains. It stimulates one's thinking."

The students liked Greer's method, too.

"Mr. Greer has a tremendous ability to handle orderly discussions, and he generates a lot of class participation and enthusiasm," explained Billy Rogers, the senior
designing engineer from the Highway Department who
attended the 1971 class.

". . . The great thing to me is the first-hand knowledge of all department policies. He might give us a
situation and say: 'We made this decision years ago
based on this information. Should we change the policy
or is the situation still valid?' "

Added John Staha, another Highway Department
engineer who took Greer's course: "It was my kind of
course because I like to ask a lot of questions. I looked
forward to every class. It is the only place in the United
States where a student can sit down and talk with a top
highway administrator and get his views on any phase of
Highway Department operations."

Dean Carlson, an assistant division engineer for the
Federal Highway Administration in Austin, another
Greer student, was "amazed" at the professor's willing-
ness to discuss such problems as how funds are allocated
to districts.

Carlson never met Greer before he entered the course,
and he was struck by the ease with which Engineer Greer
transformed himself into Professor Greer. He had heard
before he enrolled that Greer was "something less than a
warm human being." Meeting the man quickly dispelled
that myth.

"He was very personable and charming," said Carlson. "He even called me at home once to give me my
grade. There aren't many professors I ever had who
would do that. . . . Another thing, he had my term paper
published in *American Highways*, the journal for the
American Association of State Highway Officials."

After Greer was appointed by Governor Preston
Smith to become chairman of the Texas Highway Commission starting in 1969, Greer continued to teach for
three years.

It gave John German, an assistant traffic engineer for the State Highway Department, an opportunity to express his views on urban transportation to a top official.

German's term paper urged that more planning for urban areas be performed by the state agency, and he contended that cities should be awarded state funds in proportion to state taxes paid on vehicles using city streets.

Greer accepted such suggestions without commitment concerning them.

"I like the students, and I like the association with them," he remarked. "The exchange of ideas helps me in my work at the Highway Department."

He also enjoyed the opportunity to do "a little subtle recruiting" of bright students for the task of highway-building, which he loved so well.

[1] University news release, November 1967.
[2] *Texas Highways* magazine, Frank Lively, February 1971.
[3] Letter to the author, July 28, 1983.
[4] *Texas Highways* magazine, November 1967.
[5] Ibid.
[6] Ibid.

14

Mr. Chairman

"When Preston Smith appointed Dewitt Greer to the Highway Commission, it was something like appointing Winston Churchill King of England."

Reagan Houston was talking. The San Antonio banker served with Greer on the commission for six years, 1973-79, and quickly joined the cult of his admirers.

Greer's appointment to the commission came early in 1969. Greer was teaching at the University of Texas, liked what he was doing, and had considerable misgivings about returning as chairman of the governing board of the agency where he served as chief administrator for twenty-seven years.

"I tried to argue the governor out of it," Greer said of the appointment. "He said if I didn't take it, he would name (a well-known politician) to the place. It scared hell out of me, although I think he was bluffing about naming the other fellow.[1]

"I asked for a little time to think it over.

"He said 'take all the time you want — up to twenty-four hours.' "

Preston Smith gave a somewhat different version. While Greer had no idea of becoming a commission member himself, he was supporting another person for the office — certainly not the one Smith named as a threat.[2]

Smith had learned to appreciate "the capabilities of Dewitt Greer many years before I became governor of Texas."

"One of the ironic things . . . was the fact that his appointment was never particularly recognized as one that was made by me but rather the man that I succeeded in office. (John Connally retired as governor Jan. 21, 1969, and the Greer appointment became one of Smith's first official acts.)

Smith continued:

"No doubt the confusion on this came about when I personally telephoned Dewitt and asked him to visit with me in the Governor's Office. He really had no idea what the called visit concerned. When I personally asked him if he would serve, he simply said it was the greatest honor ever bestowed upon him. He promised to let me know, perhaps in a week.

"I had no idea what was holding up his decision nor did I inquire.

"In about a week, Dewitt called me and requested an appointment. He was invited over as soon as he could conveniently arrive. Within an hour, he was in the Governor's Office and agreed to accept the appointment. He said this opportunity to serve as a member of the commission was kind of like icing on the cake."

The governor asked why Greer took so long with his reply.

"He told me something so typical of the kind of gentleman he was," Smith said.

"He told me the reason he did not accept immediately was because he was committed to another man who wanted to be appointed, and before he would take the appointment it would be necessary to be released from his commitment. In other words, as was always with Dewitt Greer, he never went back on his word or a promise."

On April 1, 1969, Greer became a member of the commission in a ceremony at the State Highway Building. It was a joyous occasion, attended by many top state officials and department staff members.

Smith designated Greer as chairman, and added levity to the occasion by naming him an "Admiral of the Texas Navy," an honorary title bestowed in years past by governors on friends and prominent citizens.

The governor praised retiring Chairman J. H. Kultgen of Waco: "It is his kind that make communities great."[3]

Kultgen commented that one of the rewards of the office was meeting "wonderful people all over the state" while traveling almost 200,000 miles on official business.

As usual, Greer's response was brief:

"Texas has given me an opportunity to serve my fellow man. I pledge my efforts as a highway commissioner to continue working to give Texas a highway system of the first class."

Greer continued teaching at the university for three more years.

Although Greer probably knew more about highways than any man alive, he was meticulous to stay within the bounds of a commission member's obligation — that is, to make policy and leave the construction and maintenance authority to the state highway engineer and his staff.

His successors as state highway engineer attest how well he lived up to this goal.

J. C. Dingwall, after years as Greer's first assistant chief administrator, was head of the department when Greer returned as a commission member. There was little difference in their views on how department affairs should be conducted.

B. L. (Luther) DeBerry, who succeeded Dingwall in 1973, noted that Greer made the transition from engineer to commission chairman and "didn't interfere with the department at all — strictly policy."

DeBerry added that Greer told him he wanted to know if he (Greer) ever "got over on my side" of authority, but it never happened.

The same went for Mark G. Goode, who succeeded DeBerry in 1980.

So firmly had Greer etched his mark during his career as state highway engineer that the policies he set largely remained intact.

"Today's department is firmly rooted in the basic philosophy of D. C. Greer," Goode commented. "We intend to carry out and maintain these basic concepts."[4]

Greer did put his knowledge and expertise concerning the department to work in directing new members on the commission.

Reagan Houston, not yet on the commission, first met Greer at a weekend gathering at Dolph Briscoe's Catarina Ranch in the late 1960s.

"It was my impression at the time that he was rather shy," Houston recalled. "But as I came to know him better I would have recognized that his shyness was really an indication that he would rather have been somewhere else."[5]

Early in 1973, after Briscoe's election as governor, Houston was asked to accept appointment as chairman of the Highway Commission. Greer would remain as a commission member.

Banker-lawyer Houston pondered what accepting the office would do to his private and business life, but finally accepted. He knew relatively little about highway affairs.

Partly because of Greer's assistance, Houston said his years on the Highway Commission "became one of my most pleasant experiences."

After Houston was sworn in as commission member-chairman, Greer escorted him from a luncheon at the

Governor's Mansion to the Highway Building — Houston's first visit ever to the place.

"He commenced what was to be an extended indoctrination of the most pleasant sort," said Houston.

"I soon realized I was dealing with probably the most unselfishly dedicated man I had ever encountered. Here was a man who had served twenty-seven years as state highway engineer, and later chairman of the Highway Commission patiently feeding information to one without any such experience who was to be his chairman."

Greer's favorite role on the Highway Commission was attending monthly meetings where delegations from around the state met with department officials to discuss road needs and plans.

"He would assume his professorial demeanor," said Houston. "I have noted that commissioners have a tendency to lecture delegations appearing at the hearings, but not Dewitt. His approach was reasoning together. Likely he would know the senior members of the delegation and remind them of how they had worked together on a certain project back in 1946. By the time he would be through, any antagonism harbored by the delegation for delay in their current projects would be abated.

"This ability was most helpful when we had little in the way of funds to meet the pressing needs of our constituents. He further recognized that these hearings were not a waste of time, as suggested by some, but were an important link between the outlying communities and the Highway Department."

After the hearings, the commission held a meeting to discuss actions on the proposals, so a letter could be sent to each group.

"Dewitt was particularly skilled in having a feel for a response that was reasonably acceptable," Houston noted.

At these post-hearing sessions, the commission also

discussed bids submitted on highway work, including staff recommendations for action.

These were mostly routine, but "Dewitt had a way of smelling out any irregularity that might have missed the staff's attention," said Houston. "His experience was such that he could put himself in the position of the contractor and come up with what inevitably was a fair solution for both sides.

"More than almost anything else this made my duties palatable. I never had one moment's doubt that any position taken by Dewitt was totally in the best interest of the state."

Houston said that differences appeared within the commission.

"They almost always revolved around his desires to keep things as they traditionally had been and my (Houston's) belief that we had to face a mobility problem of a growing society over and beyond just putting pavement under the rubber.

"I am sure that Dewitt was never enthusiastic about the Highway Department taking on Public Transportation (another state agency), which I felt was a necessity.

"While we were in agreement on withholding commission approval of the turnpike plan for the old Dallas-Fort Worth toll road, I think we differed on my stand that the existing facility should be widened and that it remain a toll road until paid out. Houston said he also supported building a toll bridge across the Houston ship channel, a project which Greer felt should be financed without tolls."

"Dewitt really didn't believe in toll roads in any form or fashion," Houston observed.

Greer's dislike for combining mass transit with highways for administration also impressed Garrett Morris, one-time commission member.[6]

"Dewitt's belief in transportation stopped where the rubber met the road," said Morris. "He did not like public transportation (as part of highways), but if it ever had to be, it had to be by bus.

"I recall the early days of Governor Briscoe's administration when the merger of the Mass Transit Department with the Highway Department was under consideration. I was off the commission, but the governor asked me to talk to the commission to see if I could get their support."

An informal session was arranged for Luther DeBerry's home, next-door to Greer's residence.

Morris said that Commissioners Greer, Herbert Petry, and Charles E. Simons were present, along with Chief Engineer DeBerry.

"I made my pitch, which took thirty or forty minutes, and I would swear Dewitt didn't blink one single time during the presentation," Morris recalled.

"Later the Good Roads Association got involved, and Dewitt accepted the idea, but I don't think he ever approved of it."

Morris attributed Greer's aversion to combining mass transit with highway problems in part to Greer's dislike of controversy.

"Mass transit is controversial. Good roads are not," Morris explained.

So great was Greer's passion for harmony in the ranks that Morris said commission meetings sometimes "took on the air of a mutual admiration society."

As state highway engineer, Greer kept "the commission occupied with their own importance" and left the running of the Highway Department to Greer and his staff, according to Morris.

The result was "a sound, consistent road program in Texas, second to none in the nation. It also resulted in economy of operations so that the state got good value for its highway dollars."

A. Sam Waldrop, an Abilene business man, served on the commission during Greer's final years in that post. So impressed was Waldrop with Greer and his contribution to Texas that he suggested the writing of this book on the great highway builder's life and experiences.

"(Greer) can say more in a few words than any one I have ever known," said Waldrop.[7]

"I recall in early meetings serving with him on the commission what a tremendous and subtle teacher he was about policies and basic beliefs on highways. His often-repeated statement of 'Put the money under the rubber' has become a great tradition in this department.

"His explanation of why the governor and legislature should not use the crutch of bonding and other indebtedness to finance highways is another philosophy. His philosophy was that bonding and such as this were political traps. The politician can spend a lot of money and vote a lot of expenses, but he doesn't have the courage to support the taxes necessary for this funding. The statesman does."

Four or five months after outgoing Governor Briscoe named Waldrop to the commission, new Governor William P. Clements, Jr., the state's first Republican governor in more than a century, designated Waldrop to serve as chairman.

Waldrop said he felt inadequate on such short experience.

"I talked to Dewitt about it and explained to him how I felt about the uncertainty of ability to handle the job.

"Dewitt said to me: 'Don't worry, Sam, I'll be your strong right arm and help you over the rough places.'

"I found him to be such a person. He helped me get the big picture in highways. Through him I learned to see the great philosophy that he had been so crucial in building to make this department one of the greatest bastions of democratic service that I know of in the United States. It has been my dedication to try to pass on what he taught me."

Waldrop considers 'Greer's greatest single achievement in his career was developing an organization based on districts "rather than keeping all of the authority and management in Austin."

Always frail-looking, but healthy for many years, Greer was reappointed by Governor Briscoe in 1975 for his final six years on the commission. By then, Greer was seventy-two years old.

Briscoe asked Chairman Houston for a recommendation on reappointing Greer. His only question concerned Greer's age and physical condition.

"Although he appeared to be extremely frail, he managed to get along pretty well," said Houston.[8]

"Dolph asked me for an opinion on a reappointment for Greer, and I responded that I didn't know how I could get along without him, but I didn't know whether his health would allow him another term.

"Dolph wisely responded that he wouldn't last if he wasn't reappointed — and so it was."

Marshall Formby quipped that Greer's respect for the value of a commissioner's opinion changed after Greer joined the governing body.

As State Highway Engineer Greer "worked around the table" with the three commission members, including Formby for a time.

"The three commissioners often came up with what I thought were good suggestions," said Formby. "Greer many times vetoed them. I used to tell him that if he or one of his engineers didn't think of something it wasn't worth a damn. He would grin.[9]

"Later, he got to be a commissioner and the shoe was on the other foot. During those years, the commissioners always made good and proper suggestions — at least that's what I always told him."

Greer's twelve years on the Highway Commission saw further progress and the enhancement of Texas' reputation for excellent highways.

Walter E. Moore, editor of the *Texas Almanac* and editorial writer for the *Dallas Morning News*, reported a conversation with a non-Texan who was well acquainted with the highway administrations of other states, as well as Texas.

178 DEWITT C. GREER

" 'You Texans don't know how lucky you are,' " said Moore's fellow-passenger on an airplane flying over a Texas highway.

" 'I supply equipment to road builders in several states. When I deal with the Texas Highway Department, there's no graft, no money under the table. But I would be ashamed to tell you about the crookedness in some other states' road construction.' "[10]

Charles E. Simons, who knew Greer throughout their careers, gave the principal credit to Greer and Gibb Gilchrist. Simons worked as a capitol news correspondent, later headed the Texas Good Roads Association staff, and served on the commission with Greer.

"We have escaped the political domination that highway departments and administrators have experienced in other states," Simons told Moore. "In many instances (this) has had a devastating effect.

"We have been able to keep competent administrators and engineers who would have been kicked out if the department had become a political football, or who would have resigned rather than remain in an outfit of questionable integrity."

Simons also credited the so-called "Good Roads" amendment to the state constitution after World War II with safeguarding the funds needed for extensive highway construction and long-range planning.

Thus, Moore pointed out, Texas advanced from what a U.S. roads official described as the nation's worst system in 1895 to the undisputed leader during the 1960s and later.

While Greer drew top honors, the men and women in the department shared the acclaim.

An endowment established by the estate of John S. Redditt of Lufkin in 1966 annually awards $1,000 each to two highway employees judged to have given the most "outstanding service to the people of the State of Texas in the State Department of Highways and Public Transportation."

The awards are named for Greer and Gilchrist. Redditt served in the Texas Senate, on the Highway Commission, and in other offices while becoming an outstanding lawyer and business man in East Texas.

The Gilchrist-Greer awards are made annually at the Highway Short Course conducted at Texas A&M.

Mrs. Lady Bird Johnson established annual cash awards for highway beautification, a role in which she became a national leader.

The first presentation in 1971 was held at LBJ State Park, across the Pedernales at Stonewall, where former President Lyndon B. Johnson and Lady Bird lived.

John Berry, maintenance construction supervisor for the Conroe highway district, received the first prize.

Commission Chairman Greer presented the former First Lady with a bouquet of yellow Texas roses, adding:

"You are a morale builder second to none in the history of the Texas Highway Department. You are an inspiration to us all."[11]

Over the years, the Texas Highway Department earned a national reputation for its beautification program, its many roadside parks, and information stations along the state's principal entry points.

In 1970, when the American Society of Civil Engineers honored Greer with a life membership award, the citation mentioned his forty-seven years as an active member and his professional achievements.

"With great vision and planning ability, he foresaw development from rural to urban based communities and moved his department in that direction. With his foresight and under his leadership, Texas has completed more interstate system mileage than any other state.

"Mr. Greer's highway safety program contributed the breakaway sign mounts, the twist-and-turn-down end guard rail, the Texas crash cushion (barrels at dangerous locations to reduce the hazard of injurious collisions) and a public information program that has reduced the state's accident rate to 25 percent of the 1935 rate.

"His beautification program has resulted in safety rest areas, scenic turnouts, and roadside planting of trees, shrubs and wildflowers. His safety, beautification and research programs have received both national and international recognition."[12]

The Highway Commission and Greer were never without problems.

In 1973, when Middle East and South American oil-producing countries (members of the Organization of Petroleum Exporting Countries) declared an embargo on shipments of petroleum to the United States, the result was near-panic to the car-conscious Americans.

Motorists lined up at filling stations to share the scarce supplies, and stations closed on days when they ran out of gasoline, caused partly by the "run" of drivers seeking to keep tanks full.

To save gasoline, the federal government decreed a maximum fifty-five-mile-per-hour speed limit. Governor Dolph Briscoe called the Legislature into a special session to comply with the federal order, authorizing the Highway Commission to set speed limits conforming to the federal mandate.

The Commission under Chairman Greer acted on a request by the governor to reduce the speed limit even before the Legislature finally passed its bill. Greer contended that a statewide policy was needed immediately, rather than leave compliance with the 55 MPH limit voluntary. The state speed limit before the reduction was 70 MPH on highways in daytime and 65 MPH at night. Various exceptions authorized lower speed limits in cities and high-traffic areas.

Many Texans, especially those in spacious West Texas, grumbled over the 55 MPH limit, because it took them so long to travel the vast distances.

Greer sympathized with this view.

"I took a dim view of the federal action," Greer said. "Time has proven that federal setting of a national speed limit is not a very good idea. At places in West Texas, a restriction to 55 MPH is foolish."[13]

Nevertheless, Greer acceded to the federal order without complaint in 1973. For one thing, nobody knew how long the boycott would last or how severe the gasoline shortage would become in the United States. For another, the federal government linked compliance by states with the federal edict with the allocation of highway funds to the state. No 55 MPH ceiling — no federal money.

As a rule, however, Greer believed the state should set highway speed limits and local governments the limits within incorporated areas.

Another task which Greer found distasteful as commission member was the merger of the state's fledgling mass transit agency with the Highway Department, under the title of "State Department of Highways and Public Transportation." While Greer never really fought the merger wanted by the governor and Legislature, he considered the problems to be separate and feared involving mass transit problems would dilute the effort to build and maintain a first-class highway system, which was his main goal in life.

While Greer termed state mass transit programs "theoretically good . . . practically they are not good."[14]

"Texans love the automobile. As long as they've got money in their pockets, you're not going to get people out of their automobiles."

So far as calling the "Highway Department" by its new "Public Transportation" title, Greer added: "I never did care for the idea. Name changing was a national trend. I still call it the 'State Highway Department.' "

While some criticized the spending so many millions of dollars on Texas' farm-to-market road system, Greer retorted: "I'm an F-M man!"

The memory remained vivid of his boyhood and youth when Texas was "in the mud," and rural residents and even townspeople were isolated during bad weather.

With all-weather roads in less-populated rural areas, farmers and ranchers found it easy to move their produce to market, send children to school, and even live in town while working the land.

In recent years, the movement seemed to be toward reviving many small towns, where families can enjoy a better quality of life, work part-time on their own small acreage outside town and often hold part-time jobs commuting to nearby cities.

Until development of Texas' statewide paved roads system, rural families moved to cities to work for wages, find better educational facilities, and more entertainment.

During Greer's lifetime, the state's population shifted from largely rural to 80 percent urban. Small farmers virtually disappeared but many families still operated large enough farms and ranches to make a living.

During his fifty-three years with the department, Greer saw highways grow from two-lanes with sharp corners and narrow rights-of-way freeways, some double-decked, with controlled access and minus traffic lights.

Most Texas highways now have 200-foot right-of-way. The interstate system goes up to 400 feet, at least four lanes divided for safety, and sometimes with greater separation over favorable terrain.

Entrances and exits were improved for safety and smoother traffic flow, highway shoulders engineered so a vehicle can get off the road more safely. Sight distances improved.

Holding up a crooked small finger on his own hand, broken while helping unload a gravel truck during his youth, Greer said manual labor on highways has largely been replaced by machinery.

Whereas the Texas Legislature, under influence of the powerful railroad lobby until the 1930s and 1940s, had restricted truck loads to 7,000 pounds, 18-wheelers today carry almost unlimited loads on Texas highways, regulated by the weight carried by each axle.

Policing of highways has changed greatly. In the 1930s, a small motorcycle-mounted highway patrol operated within the Highway Department. In 1935, it became a separate Department of Public Safety with an appointed three-member governing board and a director, fashioned after the successful organization which Gibb Gilchrist and others had helped pioneer for the Highway Department.

One disappointment during Greer's tenure on the Highway Commission was the failure to receive permission and funds to construct a new state highway headquarters building in the southwest intersection of Congress Avenue and Eleventh Street in Austin, one block west of the present headquarters.

The state owned the vacant block, which served as a parking lot except for an historic building called the "Old Lundberg Bakery" and a small park along Congress Avenue.

Texas Good Roads Association officials led the effort for the new building, which Greer and the Highway Commission wanted because of inadequate space and almost non-existent parking at the building erected in 1932-33.

The existing eight-story structure described as "a classic example of the art-deco style" of the 1930s is considered one of the most attractive owned by the state in Austin, although some of its artistry was covered by a renovation.

When the campaign for a new headquarters mounted in 1971, plans called for a twenty million dollar, eleven-story white granite building, located and landscaped to enhance the scenic attraction of the downtown area between the capitol and the Governor's Mansion.

At the time, the Highway Department alone was leasing 42,500 feet of office space in Austin outside the headquarters on eight separate locations around the city.

The project ran into objections from the Austin Heritage Society, which owned the historic bakery, operated as a lunch-room and crafts store. Environmentalists complained the new highway building would be taller than the capitol. Legislative budget writers originally approved funds for the project and then backed away.

In an effort to settle the controversy and remove the vacant land from the Highway Department's control, legislators approved $1.5 million for the Parks and Wildlife Department to establish a park on the site. This failed also, when Governor Preston Smith vetoed the appropriation. The mostly paved block still serves primarily as a parking lot.

Greer's second term on the commission ended Feb. 15, 1981. After his long association with the Highway Department was over, he was honored by having the handsome old headquarters named for him, an unprecedented dedication of a state building to a living person.

The action was directed by the Texas Legislature, and a ceremony held for placing the sign: "Dewitt C. Greer State Highway Building" on the lawn outside the entrance.

The inscription on a plaque inside the building says:

"In more than fifty years of service to the people of Texas, Dewitt C. Greer contributed immeasurably to the development of the Texas highway system, and his influence is reflected in the highways of other states and nations."

The man contributed much more than good highways to Texas. He set the highest example for integrity, devotion to duty, and esteem for his fellow man.

When Greer started as state highway engineer in 1940, its annual budget was thirty-six million dollars. When he retired from that position in 1967, it was $547 million. Greer had supervised the spending of nearly five billion dollars without scandal and with outstanding results for the money — the largest construction program in the history of the world.

[1] Interview, Jan. 5, 1983, in Austin.
[2] Letter to the author, Aug. 2, 1983.
[3] *Texas Contractor* magazine, 1969.
[4] Letter to the author, July 29, 1983.
[5] Letter to the author, Apr. 20, 1983.
[6] Letter to the author, Feb. 1, 1983.
[7] Letter to the author, Mar. 18, 1983.
[8] Letter to the author, Apr. 30, 1983.
[9] Letter to the author, Mar. 8, 1983.
[10] *Dallas News*, Nov. 25, 1971.
[11] Department files, November 1971.
[12] ASCE release, St. Louis, Oct. 20, 1970.
[13] Greer interview, October 1983.
[14] Ibid.

15

The Legacy

"I'm flattered, I'm honored, I'm embarrassed. I share this honor equally with all you good people who work and have worked in the department.

"Mr. Chairman, I spent most of my career working, not talking, and that's the way it should be ended."[1]

This constituted the farewell address by Dewitt C. Greer to the career which he followed with such distinction.

The place was the hearing room of the Texas Highway Building, being renamed the "Dewitt C. Greer State Highway Building" on October 21, 1981.

It was a day marked with nostalgia, attended by about two hundred old friends and relatives of Greer.

Including Greer, nine of the guests had service totaling 435 years with the Texas department. The others introduced were former Engineer-Directors Dingwall and DeBerry, long-time Commission Secretary Clara Bewie, and retirees Bessie Bergstrom (the first employee of the department founded in 1917), Hazel Bergstrom, Archie Christian, M. V. (Bim) Greer, George Pendergrass, and Horace Warren.

"A remarkable record of distinguished service," said Commission Chairman Robert Dedman of Dallas.

Engineer-Director Goode presented Greer with a memento of the old building — a plaque of materials once part of its decor, including key No. 46 to the door of offices Greer used as department head and commissioner.

"Mr. Greer, this plaque represents only a small part of this building, but a very large part of our hearts," said Goode.

Commissioner A. Sam Waldrop of Abilene noted that the building had housed hundreds of skilled and dedicated employees, but "none has been as singularly public-service-minded and devoted to solving the highway needs of Texas as Dewitt Greer."

Unveiling the fourteen-foot limestone marker on the lawn, Chairman Dedman recited from Henry Wadsworth Longfellow's "A Psalm of Life":

> Lives of great men all remind us
> We can make our lives sublime,
> And, departing, leave behind us
> Footprints on the sands of time.

For Dewitt Greer, one might add the "footprints" are more than seventy thousand miles of all-weather highways for the benefit of travelers in his lifetime and beyond.

Greer's retirement brought another round of accolades from admirers around the state.

"In Texas, the name Dewitt C. Greer means a lot of things — from the father of the state highway system considered to be the world's best to public service unequaled for decency and achievement," wrote Felix R. McKnight.[2]

"And if this reads like a love story — a newspaper guy speaking for grateful Texas motorists — mission accomplished."

McKnight described Greer as "one of the outstanding Texans" of a period which produced two presidents, two vice presidents, two speakers of the U.S. House of Representatives, cabinet members and many others nationally noted luminaries.

Greer accomplished a highway building program which McKnight said looked like "Mission Impossible" in the 1940s.

"It involved stretches from Texarkana to El Paso and from the Panhandle to the Rio Grande Valley — with all the fingers in between," the veteran observer continued.

"He jealously guarded hundreds of millions of dollars in the highway fund with honesty and skill that produced a superior piece of highway for every dollar in the till. Texas roads became the model for the nation, for the world. Engineers came from everywhere to sit at the desk of Dewitt Greer and learn his 'touch.' The 'touch' was knowledge, work integrity."

Characteristically, Greer declined to discuss in depth any ideas or opinions on future needs in Texas highway development — for fear this might be construed as "second guessing" his successors who have borne the responsibility or who will fill the leadership role later.

Some of his long-range thoughts were expressed during his active years, however.

In 1967, his final year as department head, Greer did forecast some ideas on the subject.

Speaking on the "Next Fifty Years in Civil Engineering" to Texas members of the American Society of Civil Engineers meeting in San Antonio, Greer foresaw the impact of automation on the Motor Age.

While vehicles can be engineered to travel safely at speeds up to two hundred miles an hour, Greer declared human factors severely limit this prospect.

"Human vision and human reflexes simply are not equal to the task of traveling safely on existing highways at speeds far greater than they are set today (then 70 MPH was the legal limit).[3]

"The answer appears to rest in that dependable nostrum of our age, automation. The skeptics of today might say that the human driver will never be replaced by a mechanical gadget, but this turnabout seems inevitable."

During Greer's career, television-scan guidance systems were installed to help regulate the traffic flow on urban freeways. Interstate systems, as he predicted in 1963, were built so vehicles can go from the Atlantic to the Pacific, or almost so, without any traffic lights or cross-traffic.

Greer recalled estimates on the development of highway traffic during his lifetime had been woefully conservative.

The number of vehicles on the road in 1963 proved to be more than double the total experts predicted only a quarter-century earlier.

Better highway materials are constantly being developed, Greer noted. Included are petrochemicals to stabilize road bases, use of chemicals and electricity to reduce icing on bridges, prestressed concrete and lightweight materials to replace bulky truss bridges of yesteryear.

"You can see the dramatic strides that have been made in one generation," Greer said. "It's foolish to suppose that, in this age of fantastic technological advances, the future will be any less dramatic!"

While Greer noted long ago the experiments on electronically guided vehicles along high-speed highways and on such innovations as replacing wheeled automobiles with vehicles riding air cushions, he concluded: ". . . no development now on the drawing boards seems to preclude the need for surface travelways as far ahead as we can now see."

While the number of vehicles and miles traveled continues to increase steadily in the United States, one little-foreseen development has handicapped efforts to finance highway improvements according to Greer's hope of motor fuel taxes raising enough money to meet construction and maintenance requirements.

The rapid growth of high-mileage, small cars has cut into gasoline tax revenues, in contrast with former years when purchasers favored larger, more powerful machines.

Inflation also has cut deeply into the mileage of highways that could be built with available money.

"Road user" tax revenues still increase slowly, but cannot keep pace with the needs of a fast-growing state and car-oriented public.

The Texas Highway Commission in 1983 recommended doubling the five cent per gallon state gasoline tax, as did the Texas Municipal League. The increase, if approved by the Legislature and governor, would add an estimated $500 million annually for highway construction and maintenance.

The federal government in 1983 increased the federal levy from four cents per gallon to nine cents. But Texas Good Roads/Transportation Association officials said the expected addition in federal funds — to more than $800 million annually — still would be adequate to care for only 20,000 miles of the 73,000-mile Texas system which faced deterioration after decades of hard use and growing demands.

By the year 2000, according to the "Texas 2000" study commission, the state's population is expected to reach twenty-two million, compared to 14.3 million in 1980.

The commission predicts that Texans will continue to love their automobiles and that the highway transportation system will be sorely strained.

Lieutenant Governor Bill Hobby rates transportation as Texas' largest problem for government to solve, next to education.[4]

Highways are generally considered to have a twenty-year life span, but most of the Texas system is reaching that age, or beyond.

The Texas highway system, still considered the nation's best, "is slowly going down the drain" unless steps are taken immediately to rehabilitate deteriorating portions.[5]

That is the opinion of Dr. Frank B. McCullough, director of the Center for Transportation Research at the University of Texas at Austin.

Dr. McCullough declared Texas' phenomenal economic growth depended on the highway system which stood as "second to none in the world."

"Unfortunately, highways are much like arteries in the human body," the engineer continued. "They are taken for granted except when a blood clot or sediment stops the flow and the artery no longer functions.

". . . We will have to pay now or pay later."

Dr. McCullough added that "paying later" would be a very expensive and undesirable alternative.

The problem is immediate. Engineer-Director Goode predicted the Highway Department faced a deficit as early as July 1984 unless more money is received. The first step would be reduction of mowing along rights-of-way, which costs millions of dollars annually. State highway officials requested a $5.6 billion budget from the Legislature in 1983 for the next two years, but received $3.9 billion.

A study for the Texas Good Roads/Transportation Association reported the state needed to spend at least $1.7 billion to repair more than 10,000 miles of obsolete highway. It estimated more than $400 million in property damage and medical expenses results annually from conditions on outdated Texas highways.[6]

The prospects and the problems of highway construction, maintenance, and usage are as mind-boggling as when young Dewitt Greer joined the department in 1927, and the gargantuan solution which he engineered after World War II.

Former commission member Waldrop estimated Texas needs to raise and spend more than sixty billion dollars (in terms of 1982 dollars) during the next twenty years to keep the system up to date.

The challenge is as real, and in some ways greater than when Dewitt Greer took command of the highway department in 1940.

Texas did *not* build the greatest system of roads the world has ever known because of its vibrant economy. Rather, the state's great economic growth largely followed its good roads.

For this, the public can thank Dewitt Greer more than any other person. He was the director, architect-engineer — a leader of vision, ability, and integrity.

[1] *Transportation News*, November-December 1981.
[2] *Dallas Times-Herald*, July 26, 1981.
[3] THD files.
[4] *Dallas News*, Kathryn Baker, Jan. 2, 1983.
[5] University of Texas News Service, Feb. 24, 1983.
[6] *Austin American-Statesman*, Sept. 28, 1983.

INDEX

About the Author

Richard Morehead was born November 16. 1913, at Plainview in Hale County, Texas, and attended Plainview public schools. Later educational opportunities included Wayland College, the University of Missouri, and the University of Texas at Austin, where he received the Bachelor of Journalism degree in 1935.

Morehead served as reporter for the *Plainview Herald* during the summer of 1933 and 1934, the *Daily Texan* from 1933 to 1935, and the United Press (International) from 1935-1942. He was the *Dallas News Austin* bureau correspondent from 1942 to 1978, and bureau chief from 1965-1979.

Morehead has been a participant in the American Press Institute, a national seminar on political writing, and a winner the SMU Southwest Journalism Forum award for political writing. He also has ceived a UPI award, was three times winner of the Headliner Club award (based civil rights-education reporting).

He is a member and past president of the Society of Professional Journal Sigma Delta Chi, Austin Professional Chapter, and a member and former natic director of the Association of Petroleum Writers.

.

www.ingramcontent.com/pod-product-compliance
Lightning Source LLC
Chambersburg PA
CBHW060757100426

42813CB00004B/857